# POWER POINTS!

# POWER POINTS!

## How to Design and Deliver Presentations That Sizzle and Sell

### HARRY MILLS

**AMACOM**
American Management Association
New York • Atlanta • Brussels • Chicago • Mexico City • San Francisco
Shanghai • Tokyo • Toronto • Washington, D.C.

Special discounts on bulk quantities of AMACOM books are available to corporations, professional associations, and other organizations. For details, contact Special Sales Department, AMACOM, a division of American Management Association, 1601 Broadway, New York, NY 10019.
Tel: 212-903-8316. Fax: 212-903-8083.
E-mail: specialsls@amanet.org
Website: www.amacombooks.org/go/specialsales
To view all AMACOM titles go to: www.amacombooks.org

This publication is designed to provide accurate and authoritative information in regard to the subject matter covered. It is sold with the understanding that the publisher is not engaged in rendering legal, accounting, or other professional service. If legal advice or other expert assistance is required, the services of a competent professional person should be sought.

Mills, Harry

Power points! : how to design and deliver presentations that sizzle and sell / Harry Mills.
    p.   cm.
   Includes bibliographical references and index.
   ISBN-13: 978-0-8144-7469-3
   ISBN-10: 0-8144-7469-1
   1. Business presentations.   2. Microsoft PowerPoint (Computer file)   I. Title.

HF5718.22.M55   2007
658.4′52—dc22

                                2006036988

Printing number

10  9  8  7  6  5  4  3  2  1

# CONTENTS

# THE COMPANION CD-ROM

Harry Mills with PresentationPro—one of the world's leading PowerPoint design teams—created and designed the model PowerPoint slideshows and templates.

*Slideshows*

1. **Planning for the Perfect Performance:**
   How to Organize a Persuasive Presentation

2. **Visual Magic:**
   How to Create Stunning Visuals—That Sell, Motivate and Persuade

3. **Wooing with Color:**
   How to Use Color to Enhance, Motivate and Persuade

4. **Deliver with Style:**
   How to Present with Flair and Impact

5. **Stunning Graphics:**
   How to Put the Wow into Pie, Bar, and Line Graphs

6. **Dazzling Diagrams:**
   How to Inform with Impact

7. **The Ultimate Sales Presentation:**
   How to Persuade with Punch, Power, and Pizzazz

*PresentationPro Templates, Graphics, and Icons*

Thirty professional PowerPoint high-impact templates, graphics, and icons designed by PresentationPro. Go to www.presentation pro.com.

The slideshows provide:

- A series of practical, visual lessons on how to plan, design, and deliver persuasive PowerPoints.

- Vivid examples of how spectacular and persuasive PowerPoint can be, with the help of imaginative design.

# ACKNOWLEDGMENTS

This book would have never been completed without the urging and support of the PresentationPro team. Craig White provided the drive and urging to write a book that would show presenters how to present and deliver what Craig calls killer presentations.

Randall Lok and Kelly Ellis have used their design talents to give *Power Points!* added visual impact.

# INTRODUCTION

In the early 1990s, I delivered what I believed was a motivating and persuasive speech to a Toyota conference. The stories went down well, the message seemed compelling.

So I was taken aback when one of Toyota's senior executives asked me why I hadn't used PowerPoint—like the rest of the conference presenters. I snapped back: "Lincoln didn't use PowerPoint at Gettysburg. Can you imagine Churchill using PowerPoint to rally the British House of Commons after the evacuation at Dunkirk?"

I now believe Churchill and Lincoln, if alive today, would use PowerPoint given the right circumstances. Both Churchill and Lincoln relished using new technologies.

As speakers, Churchill and Lincoln practiced the three-part rule of classic rhetoric: (1) start with an attention-grabbing introduction; (2) use the body of your speech to deliver persuasive content; and (3) finish on a strong note with a call to action.

If alive today, Churchill and Lincoln would have readily grasped the fact that PowerPoint is not an alternative to great speaking. PowerPoint is simply a multimedia speaker support tool to be used where speech plus multimedia works better than speech alone.

Moreover, Churchill and Lincoln would have intuitively grasped that PowerPoint presentations work best when organized using the three-part classic presentation formula. In other words, Churchill and Lincoln would plan and structure their PowerPoint presentations in three parts.

What Churchill and Lincoln would have had to learn was how to use and exploit the multimedia capabilities of PowerPoint.

They would have had to learn to think like director Steven Spielberg. Spielberg is a master of the big screen because he understands how to tell a great story with pictures and dialogue.

PowerPoint does some things spectacularly well, and some things much less well. As an economical, easy-to-use visual persuader, it is unequaled. The trouble is, unskilled presenters use PowerPoint's ability to quickly produce text slides that drown us in a tidal wave of bullet text.

As well as understanding technology issues, PowerPoint presenters have to cope with limitations imposed by the way our brain works. Our short-term memory can only hold a very limited amount of information at one time. The brain processes presentations through two channels; a visual channel and an auditory channel. Overload one or both of these channels and you have PowerPoint overload. We've all witnessed the symptoms. Audiences start suffering from MEGO (**M**ine **E**yes **G**laze **O**ver) syndrome.

In *Power Points!* we show you how to align your PowerPoint presentations with the way the brain works, which in practice means optimizing how we use both auditory and visual channels.

There never has been a better time for presenters to reassess how they use PowerPoint to persuade, inform and inspire. Microsoft Office PowerPoint 2007 takes visual presentations to a new plane.

You really can create high-impact, dynamic presentations without the help of a design professional. PowerPoint 2007's new graphics program even allows you to transform a bulleted list into a diagram.

So would a twenty-first century Churchill or Lincoln use a PowerPoint presentation to make a three-minute motivational speech? I think not. Would they use a PowerPoint to argue for a change of military strategy to a group of assembled generals? I think so! Try using words to describe accurately the battle plans for a D-Day invasion. You can't. You need maps, diagrams, pictures and tables. And that's where PowerPoint is unmatched.

As a speaker, I still love delivering Churchillian or Lincoln-style speeches. However, as a professional persuader who has authored books such as Artful Persuasion: *How to Command Attention, Change Minds and Influence People,* I make my day-to-day living helping companies shape mission-critical presentations for big sales, product launches and major deals.

# POWER POINTS!

**PART ONE**

STAND AND DELIVER:

THE SEVEN STEPS TO

PRESENTATION SUCCESS

# The Seven Steps to Presentation Success

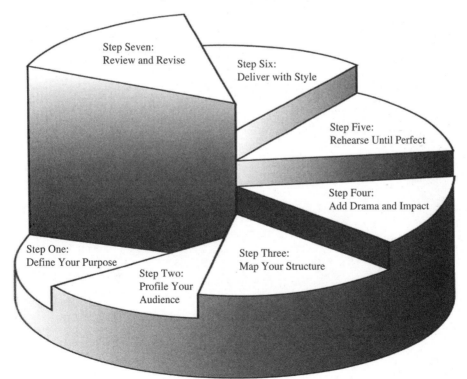

Step Seven:
Review and Revise

Step Six:
Deliver with Style

Step Five:
Rehearse Until Perfect

Step Four:
Add Drama and Impact

Step One:
Define Your Purpose

Step Two:
Profile Your
Audience

Step Three:
Map Your Structure

All presentations, whether delivered primarily as a speech or as a PowerPoint, go through the same seven steps.

**Step 1: Define Your Purpose.** The first question every presenter has to determine is, Why am I presenting? Is it to inform, entertain or persuade?

**Step 2: Profile Your Audience.** You should always analyze your audience's needs and motivations.

**Step 3: Map Your Structure.** Presenting is essentially storytelling. And all good stories need structure.

**Step 4: Add Drama and Impact.** Even the most boring factual presentation needs livening up with anecdotes, stories or captivating visuals.

**Step 5: Rehearse Until Perfect.** The more you rehearse, the better you get.

**Step 6: Deliver with Style.** The way you deliver is as, if not more, important than your content.

**Step 7: Review and Revise.** The best presenters learn from their mistakes by continually evaluating their performance.

"There will be six designated yawning breaks during
my presentation. Please pace your boredom accordingly."

# CHAPTER ONE

# STEP ONE:
# DEFINE YOUR PURPOSE

· · · · · · · · · · · · ·

*"A speech without a specific purpose is like a journey without a destination."*

—RALPH C. SMEDLEY

Before you deliver any presentation, you need to determine your primary purpose. Ask:

● Is it to inform?

● Is it to entertain?

● Is it to persuade?

Your primary purpose should influence the tone, content and structure of your presentation.

## ESTABLISHING FOCUS

### Determine Your Purpose

Great speakers create focus by starting with a clear purpose. The purpose of your speech is what you want your audience to

> "I stand in pause where
> I shall first begin."
> —WILLIAM SHAKESPEARE

remember and do as a result of hearing you. No one should ever leave a presentation of yours without knowing your purpose.

### Inform, Persuade, or Entertain?

Are you speaking to persuade, inform or entertain? How you want to move your audience should be central to your approach. Even though we should identify each purpose separately, they often overlap. For example, you may want to inform and entertain at the same time.

| PURPOSE | AIM |
| --- | --- |
| To persuade | To change or reinforce an attitude, belief or behavior |
| To inform | To share new information |
| To entertain | To amuse with humor and anecdotes |

## HOT TIPS

- **Ask "What do I want my audience to know or feel?"** Every part of your speech will be influenced by the answer to this question.

- **Keep your purpose specific.** Focus on exactly what you want your listeners to do when you finish speaking.

  - **Vague:** *My purpose is to tell the board about the new plans.*
  - **Specific:** *My purpose is to persuade the board to fund the new export drive to China.*

- **Always use titles.** A sharp, punchy title will help you clarify your purpose.

  - **Title:** *Speed kills*
  - **Purpose:** *To make drivers slow down*

- **Analyze your audience.** The purpose of your speech should always be tailored precisely to your audience's needs.

- **Write out a one-sentence summary of your speech.** If your purpose is clear, you should be able to summarize your key message.

## PRESENTING TO INFORM

### Purpose

An informative speech or PowerPoint presentation delivers fresh information. An informative presentation must always:

> "There is nothing so uncertain and slippery as fact."
> —SARA COLERIDGE

- Grab and hold your audience's interest.

- Get the audience to retain your key points.

### Use New and Useful Information

An informative presentation always should contain new and useful information. There is nothing more boring than listening to recycled, time-worn material. The information has to be fresh, practical and relevant.

### Structure for Retention

An informative presentation must help the audience retain and remember information.

An informative presentation must be built on a strong, logical, clear sequence of ideas, and the points must be presented in an easy-to-remember pattern.

### Speech or PowerPoint Presentation?

If you have a lot of data to present and retention is critical, then PowerPoint is the ideal tool. The challenge is not to overwhelm your audience with too much information presented too quickly.

## HOT TIPS

- **Motivate your audience to listen.** In your introduction, sell the benefits of the information you have to offer.

- **Keep selling the benefits of listening.** During your presentation, keep relating your material back to your audience's needs and desires.

- **Arouse interest with a provocative question, anecdote or startling statistic.** A simple question, such as: "How would you like to double your profits in six months?" will give you the attention grabber you need to establish interest.

- **Present your information in small, digestible chunks.** Build your presentation around the three to five key points you want the audience to remember. Hand out a summary of your slides and notes. Supporting handouts are a breeze to create in PowerPoint.

- **Use repetition to hammer home your key points.** Repeat your key messages several times using different words, pictures, and stories.

## PRESENTING TO ENTERTAIN

### The Fear of Failure

> "Once you've got people laughing, they're listening and you can tell them almost anything."
> —HERBERT GARDNER

The most difficult challenge for most presenters is to entertain an audience. Most of us are terrified at standing before a critical audience after a joke has failed. The resulting embarrassment has numbed some of history's greatest speakers.

### The Biggest Myth About Humor

Most people wrongly believe humor is an innate skill; either you have it or you don't. To entertain and use humor well you don't have to be a comedian. You don't even have to be able to tell a joke.

"The most serious people in the world use humor," says presidential speech-writer Peggy Noonan. "Humor is gracious and it shows respect. It shows the audience you think enough of them to want to entertain them."

### Communicate a Sense of Humor

The key to success is to appreciate the difference between being funny and displaying a sense of humor. If you have a sense of humor, then you can be entertaining.

### Speech or PowerPoint Presentation?

If your primary purpose is to entertain, it is usually best to stay away from PowerPoint. If you have to use PowerPoint, replace your bullets with key statements and visuals.

### HOT TIPS

- **Always link humor to a point in your presentation.** If you use humor to make a point, you will rarely, if ever, fail.

- **Don't use pointless jokes.** The biggest mistake is to use irrelevant jokes that have nothing to do with the main point of the presentation.

- **Use non-joke humor.** If you can't tell jokes, use personal anecdotes, analogies, and quotes.

- **Write your serious message first.** Then use humor to support your key points.

- **Poke fun at yourself.** Most great speakers use self-effacing humor to build rapport.

- **Start with short, punchy stories.** They're much easier to master. A seventy-five-word tale takes about thirty seconds to deliver.

- **If you are using PowerPoint,** replace all your words and bullet points with visuals. Use cartoons, humorous clip art, and provocative photos.

## PRESENTING TO PERSUADE

### What is Persuasion?

> "To be persuasive, we must be believable. To be believable, we must be credible. To be credible, we must be truthful."
>
> —EDWARD R. MURROW

The most common purpose of communication is to persuade. Your goal is to change or reinforce an attitude, belief, or behavior.

### The Credibility Formula

When persuaders lack credibility we discount everything they say: To persuade, we must be believable, and to be believable, we must be credible. Credibility rests on two pillars: trust and expertise. Think of credibility as a formula: Trust + Expertise = Credibility.

### Use Logic and Evidence

Persuasion is built on a foundation of structure, logic, and reason. The rational mind looks for structure and order supported by concrete evidence. Professionals such as engineers will hunt for any flaw in your logic, so beware!

### Use Emotion

People are often not influenced by the true facts of a situation. More often they are influenced by what makes the most vivid impression. Tapping emotional needs is central to successful persuasion.

## Speech or PowerPoint Presentation?

If you have a small amount of data to communicate and you can get your point across in five minutes or less then a speech is likely to be more persuasive. For longer, data-heavy presentations such as business cases, PowerPoint works best.

## HOT TIPS

- **Think: WIIFM.** People want to know, What's In It For Me? Analyze your audience's basic needs before you present. Ask:

  - What do they stand to gain from my proposal?
  - What do they stand to lose from my proposal?

- **Highlight the benefits.** Continually sell the advantages of your products or services. Don't get bogged down in the facts or features of your proposal.

- **Present both sides of a debate.** Two-sided messages generally work best, especially with those who know there are opposing arguments.

- **Call for action.** At the end of your presentation tell your audience what you want them to do.

- **Use fear as a motivator.** Of all our emotions, fear is possibly the most powerful motivator. Fear of loss is usually a more powerful motivator than the prospect of future gains. But use it cautiously—without overkill.

- **Don't exaggerate or oversell your case, especially when talking to professionals.** The audience will discount everything you say.

"Before I begin, I'd just like to make it known
that I didn't volunteer to do this presentation."

# CHAPTER TWO

# STEP TWO: PROFILE YOUR AUDIENCE

. . . . . . . . . . . .

"The best audience is intelligent, well educated and a little drunk."

—ALBEN W. BARKLEY

Audiences range from the overwhelmingly supportive to the actively hostile. Presenting to a hostile group requires a very different persuasion strategy from presenting to a supportive audience.

## ANALYZING YOUR AUDIENCE

### Tailor Your Strategy

There are at least six different types of audiences and each one requires a different persuasion strategy.

> "There is no director who can direct you like an audience."
>
> —FANNY BRICE

### The Six Audience Types

1. The **hostile** audience disagrees with you and may even be working actively against you.

2. The **neutral** audience understands your position but still needs convincing.

3. The **uninterested** audience is informed about the issues you want to discuss but doesn't care at all.

4. The **uninformed** audience lacks the information it needs to be convinced.

5. The **supportive** audience already agrees with you.

6. The **mixed** audience contains a cross-section of differing attitudes and views.

## The Three Key Questions

To work out your audience type, ask these three questions:

**Knowledge:** What does my audience know about the topic I want to talk about?

**Interest:** How interested is the audience in my subject?

**Support:** How much support already exists for my views?

## Audience Analysis Template

Audience's major concerns _____

Theme of meeting _____

Knowledge of topic _____

Interest in topic _____

Support for views _____

Occupations/roles _____

Education levels _____

Age, sex, ethnic backgrounds _____

Religion/political persuasion _____

# INFLUENCING A HOSTILE AUDIENCE

### Your Toughest Challenge

The hostile audience disagrees with your proposals. They are your toughest challenge. They feel just as strongly as you do, but they hold opposing opinions. Because of your differences they will question your credibility and openmindedness.

> "If you can't convince 'em, confuse 'em."
> —HARRY S. TRUMAN

### Create Rapport

First, a hostile audience has to be "warmed up" to the point where they will listen to you and consider your points. Poking fun at yourself is often a good way to start.

### Build Credibility

Take every opportunity to demonstrate your expertise. Cite experts whom the audience respects, even if they are not your first choice. Be scrupulously fair when citing facts and statistics.

### Don't Ask For Too Much

Stress that you are looking for a win-win outcome rather than a win-lose solution. Don't expect major shifts in attitude. Ask for a little and get it rather than asking for a lot and facing rejection. Remember, if you neutralize a hostile audience, you've made progress.

## HOT TIPS

- **Don't start with a direct attack.** You will lose your audience and very likely increase their hostility.

- **Start with humor or a story.** They are good ways to build initial rapport.

- **Focus first on the areas of agreement.** Stress these before delving into areas of conflict.

- **Back up every claim you make with rock-solid evidence.** Where there is doubt, understate your claims. Source all references to prove your fairness.

- **Avoid hypothetical examples.** Make sure all your case studies and stories are representative and drawn from real life.

- **Don't tell your audience you plan to change their minds.** It will simply antagonize them and harden their resistance.

## INFLUENCING A NEUTRAL AUDIENCE

### Create a Connection

> "Use soft words and hard arguments."
> —ENGLISH PROVERB

Neutral audiences neither support nor oppose you. They understand the issue but feel no connection and have yet to be converted. They are indifferent. The first task is to create a link between your proposal and the needs of the audience. Start by spelling out the benefits of your proposition by linking these benefits to the interests of your audience.

### Be Likeable

Likeable communicators are more influential. We try to please people we like and find attractive.

### Keep It Simple

Limit your points to three clear, compelling messages. Back them up with expert testimony, quotes, statistics and case studies. Draw heavily on concrete examples that are familiar to your audience.

### Point Out the Downside

Don't forget to point out the downside of not accepting your proposals. Alert your audience to any competitor or common enemies who might take advantage of their inaction.

## HOT TIPS

- **Use stories, personal anecdotes and analogies to create an emotional link.** The neutral audience first needs to be emotionally linked to your proposal.

- **Highlight any similarities you share with the audience.** Similarities deepen trust and rapport.

- **Don't drown them in data.** The neutral audience already understands the issue. They simply need to be converted.

- **Present both sides of any debates.** Demonstrate your fairness by acknowledging other points of view.

- **Stress that what you want to do is popular.** People like to follow what is standard practice or part of a trend.

- **Associate your proposals with successful people.** Search out organizations and people your audience admires.

## INFLUENCING AN UNINTERESTED AUDIENCE

### They Don't Care

Facing an uninterested audience is much tougher than facing a neutral one. The uninterested audience knows about your topic but doesn't care. The issues either bore them or are seen as irrelevant.

> "If you cannot get people to listen to you any other way, tell them its confidential."
> —PATRICK MURRAY

### Inspire and Motivate

The uninterested audience needs motivating and energizing. Therefore, the first task is to provide inspiration and vision.

### Provide Relevance

The second task is to make them care by showing them how the topic affects or will affect them. Show them they can't afford not to care. Spell out the benefits of becoming involved.

### Don't Ignore the Negative

After spelling out the positive benefits, point out the downside. Spell out what they stand to lose by not becoming involved. Fear is probably the most powerful motivator. Remember, fear of loss is a much more powerful motivator than the prospect of gain.

## HOT TIPS

- **Create a compelling vision.** Paint a picture of a bright future. Create relevance by linking what your audience does to a higher good.

- **Use a dramatic opening.** Start with a powerful story, a dramatic headline, or a heart-stopping fact.

- **Don't drown your audience with information.** Three to five compelling facts are usually enough. Long lists of reasons and facts will demotivate.

- **Use personalized case studies.** Personalized case studies of successful change work much better than dry statistics.

- **Use metaphors and analogies to create memorable images.** Martin Luther King's "I have a dream" speech and Churchill's "Iron Curtain" speeches are remembered because of the way they use metaphors.

## INFLUENCING AN UNINFORMED AUDIENCE

### Educate

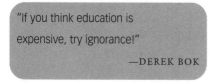

"If you think education is expensive, try ignorance!"

—DEREK BOK

The uninformed audience simply lacks information. It doesn't know enough to act, so it needs educating. Start by establishing your credibility.

### Keep It Simple

Don't bury your audience in data. Limit your presentation to a few easy-to-follow, logical points. Back these up with statistics and solid, concrete examples.

### Don't Debate Issues

Don't confuse your audience by discussing the pros and cons behind each issue. These people haven't yet formed an opinion, so they don't yet need to debate the issues. Keep your structure simple and straightforward.

### Be Interactive

Use an interactive style. Encourage the audience to ask questions throughout the presentation, and leave time for extended discussion at the end.

### Take Your Time

Allow plenty of time for people to absorb any new ideas. Give people a break and time to think about the issues before asking for action. You'll be much more successful.

## HOT TIPS

- **Start by establishing your credibility.** Showcase your expertise, experience, or qualifications.

- **Use the PEP (Point, Example, Point) formula.** Make your point, support it with a vivid example, and then remake your point.

- **Create a clear, simple structure.** Avoid complexity. Use supporting charts and visual aids where you need to explain complex ideas and processes.

- **Use analogies, models, and pictures** to explain difficult concepts.

- **Highlight and refute any common myths and misconceptions.** Common misconceptions are a major cause of misunderstanding and a barrier to learning.

- **Play down the notion that any persuasion is going on at all.** Your audience will become suspicious and resistant if you don't.

## INFLUENCING A SUPPORTIVE AUDIENCE

### Inspire and Recharge

> "You can't sweep other people off their feet, if you can't be swept off your own."
>
> —CLARENCE DAY

The supportive audience is the easiest to persuade. This is your ideal audience. Since they already agree with you, your task is to recharge them and then make sure they are committed to a plan of action.

Your first task is to refire the group's enthusiasm with an inspirational address. Reinforce their commitment with success stories and vivid testimonials.

Remind everyone what you share as a group. Stress **T.E.A.M.** (Together Everyone Achieves More). Urge audience members to support each other.

### Call for Action

If your group is actively supportive, talk about what work remains unfinished. Urge them to commit themselves to new and more ambitious goals.

Finally, hand out a detailed plan of action with clear deadlines. Don't give them a chance to procrastinate or reconsider.

### Beware of Complacency

The greatest mistake with a supportive audience is to take them for granted. Remember, even the strongest of supporters can need remotivating.

## HOT TIPS

- **Set specific, achievable goals.** Your audience has been converted. Your task is to get them to act as soon as possible.

- **Get individual audience members to publicly commit themselves to particular time-driven goals.** People are much more likely to keep promises made in public.

- **You don't have to prove your case.** With a supportive audience there is no need to present a balanced view. You are talking to committed fans.

- **Inoculate your audience against future attacks from opponents.** Anticipate and refute your opponents' possible arguments. Your audience will be armed and prepared.

- **Get the audience to share their success stories.** Supportive audiences love to hear tales of triumph over adversity from fellow believers.

## INFLUENCING A MIXED AUDIENCE

### Identify the Decision Makers

Very few audiences are all neutral or all supportive. Most audiences are mixed, made up of a spectrum of viewpoints. The key with a mixed audience is to identify who in the audience you really have to win

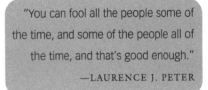

"You can fool all the people some of the time, and some of the people all of the time, and that's good enough."
—LAURENCE J. PETER

over. You have to identify which sub-group has the most power.

With a mixed audience you need to identify which sub-group has the numbers and then concentrate your efforts on the groups that count.

### Tailor Your Rewards

If you can, appeal to the different groups in your audience with different parts of your message. Look for creative ways to influence each sub-group by offering each of them a different reward.

Look at a typical snack food commercial. It promises kids a great taste while reassuring parents the snacks are healthy and nutritious.

### Enlist Your Supporters' Help

Before the presentation it sometimes pays to ask key supporters to provide you with active support during the meeting.

## HOT TIPS

- **Don't promise "everything to everyone."** If there are groups in your audience with competing sub-agendas, you may end up alienating everyone.

- **Use "glittering generalities."** Glittering generalities are "purr" words that have positive associations but are essentially ambiguous.

- **Stress common interests.** Acknowledge your differences after reminding everyone what you have in common.

- **Discuss issues not personalities.** Blame the "system" rather than the person for failures.

- **Call for positive suggestions.** Ask the audience to express any opinions in one sentence, and then to suggest something positive.

- **Don't call for a vote.** It will simply highlight the divisions. A loss could easily be catastrophic and destroy your later chances for recovery.

## SET REALISTIC AND ACHIEVABLE GOALS

Many presenters make the mistake of trying to achieve too much. For example, they try to convert an actively hostile opponent into a believer, and think they have failed when the person fails to turn into a "born again" zealot.

Full-scale conversions from active opposition to active support are relatively rare. If you neutralize a hostile person in an audience, you have been successful. They may not ever become a supporter, but the fact that they are no longer working against you must still be chalked up as a victory.

## Cognitive Consistency

One of the reasons we are resistant to making radical attitude changes is our psychological need to stay cognitively consistent. Cognitive consistency refers to our need to have consistency between any new information we take notice of and our existing attitudes: beliefs and behaviors.

## We Reject Information That Conflicts with Our Beliefs

If we hear a new message that clashes with our existing beliefs, we can argue against it and reject it, or interpret it and accept it. Normally, if the message is clear and threatening, we reject it. For example, cigarette smokers tend to reject clear evidence that cigarette smoking causes lung cancer and other diseases.

New information that challenges our existing beliefs causes stress. And the easiest way to get rid of that stress is to reject the new information or selectively reinterpret it.

"Always start your presentation with a joke,
but be careful not to offend anyone! Don't mention
religion, politics, race, money, disease, technology,
men, women, children, plants, animals, food..."

# CHAPTER THREE

# STEP THREE: MAP AND STRUCTURE YOUR STORY

• • • • • • • • • • • •

"A speech is like a love affair: Any fool can start one but to end it requires considerable skill."

—LORD MANCROFT

The art of presenting is the art of storytelling. What the ancient philosophers called rhetoric is storytelling.

The classic three-part framework—(1) tell 'em what you're going to tell them; (2) tell 'em; (3) tell 'em what you've told them—has always been the staple structure for a great speech.

The great news for presenters is that the three-part classic persuasion framework which has worked successfully for brilliant speeches since the time of Aristotle works just as well in Power-Point.

## THE THREE-PART CLASSIC PRESENTATION FORMULA

### Building Your Outline

The Mills persuasive presentation formula builds upon the classic three-part presentation framework.

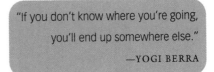

"If you don't know where you're going, you'll end up somewhere else."

—YOGI BERRA

**Part One:** The *preview* or introduction.

**Part Two:** The body or *view*. This is where you sell your point of view.

**Part Three:** The *review* or conclusion.

### Part One: Preview

Your introduction should grab your listeners' attention, sell your listeners on why they should listen, and provide an overview of what's to come.

### Part Two: View (Point of)

The body delivers the content. This is where you state your *point of view,* make three to five compelling points, and support them with evidence and illustrations.

### Part Three: Review

A strong conclusion recaps the positioning statement and key points, includes a wrap-up story, and finishes with a call for action.

The three-step preview, view, and review formula is logical, compelling, persuasive, and easy to create. It is perfect for both traditional speeches and PowerPoint presentations.

## The Three-Part Framework

**Preview**

(10-15 percent of time)

- **Hook:** Opening statement to grab attention
- **Positioning statement:** Benefit statement selling advantages of listening
- **Overview:** Key points that support positioning statement

**View (Point of)**

(80-85 percent of time)

- **Point One:** Evidence/illustration
- **Point Two:** Evidence/illustration
- **Point Three:** Evidence/illustration

**Review**

(5 percent of time)

- **Recap:** Summary of positioning statement and key points
- **Memorable conclusion:** Wrap-up story or statement
- **Call to action:** Request for order/commitment

## APPLYING THE THREE-PART FORMULA TO POWERPOINT

The classic three-part presentation framework that works so well with traditional speeches works just as well for those presenters who prefer using PowerPoint.

### What Makes PowerPoint Different?

All you have to keep in mind is what distinguishes a PowerPoint presentation from a traditional speech. The key differences are:

- PowerPoint organizes and stores ideas as slides.

- PowerPoint is a multimedia tool that allows you to use stunning visuals—graphics, charts, diagrams, photos and artwork, plus video film clips, sound effects, sound tracks, and narration.

### Three-Act Structure

Because PowerPoint is primarily a visual tool that organizes its ideas sequentially like a stage drama, we use a three-act model.

- Preview—Act I

- View—Act II

- Review—Act III

### Slide Sequences

We call each subgroup of related slides a sequence.

# Three-Act PowerPoint Presentation

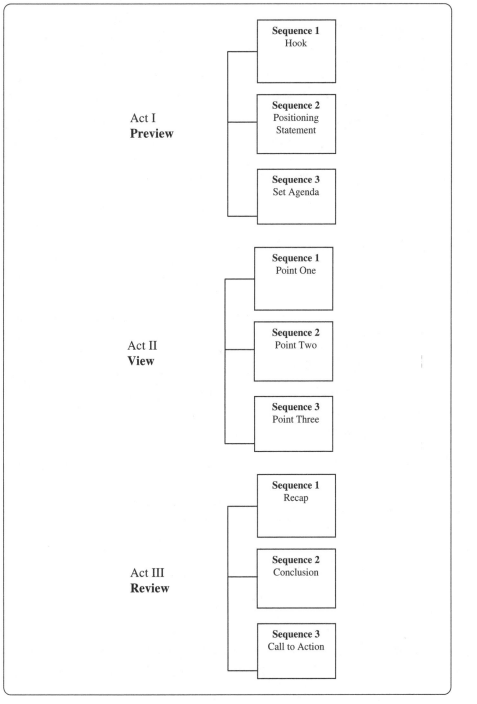

## FOCUSING YOUR PITCH

### Start with the End in Mind

> "I like the way you always state the obvious with a sense of discovery."
> —GORE VIDAL

To create focus, start by identifying your prime presentation objective or goal. First write down what do you want your audience to do or think when they leave your presentation.

### Write a Compelling Title for Your Presentation

Having defined your end point, you're ready to start drafting a short, punchy, intriguing title for your presentation. Your presentation title needs to pass three tests.

### The Three Tests

**Test One:** Does the presentation title grab the audience's attention? Or does it sound dull, bland, and boring? Short, punchy, provocative titles work best.

**Test Two:** Does the presentation title tap into the audience's prime interest? Ask what interest already exists in the minds of the audience.

**Test Three:** Does the presentation title create anticipation? The best presentation titles generate curiosity and intrigue by offering a benefit for listening that is tangible and believable.

When you have a presentation title that passes these three tests you have one of the foundations for a great presentation.

### HOT TIPS

- **Keep drafting and redrafting your presentation title until it is word perfect.** Then test your presentation on a cross section of your target audience.

Here is how the title for the PowerPoint presentation that inspired this book emerged.

| FIRST DRAFT | COMMENT |
|---|---|
| Advanced Presentation Skills | Bland and boring. |

| SECOND DRAFT | COMMENT |
|---|---|
| Power Points!<br>How to Present with Punch and Pizzazz | Subtitle reads well but lacks specificity. |

| FINAL DRAFT | COMMENT |
|---|---|
| Power Points!<br>How to Design and Deliver Presentations that Sizzle and Sell | Subtitle is specific and spells out benefits of the book. |

## USE COMPELLING HEADLINES TO CREATE FLOW AND DIRECTION

### Titles vs. Headlines

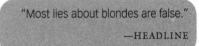

"Most lies about blondes are false."
—HEADLINE

It's very common to find a slide title such as "Distribution and Revenue Projections" as the heading in a PowerPoint slide. Titles such as these tell you (the presenter) where you are in your presentation, but they don't offer your audience an explanation of the key point on your slide. A headline must capture the essence of the slide. A headline should summarize the key point. A headline emphasizes the action you want to take by using active verbs.

Slide titles should also challenge your viewers to sit up and pay attention.

### The Naked Headline Test

Before you add a single bullet point or a graphic to your slide show, set your presentation up as a series of sharp headlines. Give each slide it's own headline, then display it as nothing more than a series of headlines. This headline test allows you to test your story-line for logic and flow.

Once you have a list of headlines that inform, flow, and persuade, you can add graphics and words with the comfort of knowing you are building on a logical storyline.

## HOT TIPS

- **With slide titles, give more information rather than less.**

  - **Brief:** Use Headlines
  - **Better:** Announce your key messages with headlines

- **Emphasize action.** Highlight action by using active verbs.

  - **Boring:** Implementation
  - **Better:** Action needed: purchase new hardware

- **Be specific rather than general.** Replace broad and boring concrete terms.

  - **Boring:** Background
  - **Better:** Events leading to security review

- **Include your point in your title.** Put your bottom line on top.

  - **Boring:** Recommendations
  - **Better:** Train support staff

- **Don't be afraid to phrase titles as questions.** They challenge and intrigue.

  - **Boring:** ROI

  - **Better:** What will be our return on investment?

## SELL THE SIZZLE

### WIIFM

When you are making a presentation, it always pays to remember the audience you are trying to convince is always asking "What's in it for me?" (WIIFM). You'll never convince anyone in a presentation until you can answer that question.

> "If you can't convince 'em, confuse them."
> —HARRY TRUMAN

Compare the appeal of the statement "apples contain vitamins and natural sugar" with "an apple a day keeps the doctor away." The first lists features or facts about apples; the second describes the benefits or advantages of eating apples.

### Sell the Tan Not the Sun

To keep sales people focused on benefits they are taught "sell the sizzle, not the steak," "sell the tan, not the sun," and "sell the envy, not the car."

Presentations that spell out the benefits for the audience answer the WIIFM question. Make sure you always keep the needs of your audience at the forefront of your mind.

### Losses and Gains

People respond to any given proposition for one of two reasons: to gain something they do not have or to avoid losing something they now possess. As a motivator, the fear of loss is normally twice as powerful as the prospect of gain.

## HOT TIPS

- **To identify your audience's primary motivators, ask what they stand to gain or stand to lose by taking advantage of what is being proposed in the presentation.** Remember, fear of loss is a more powerful motivator than the prospect of gain.

- **During the presentation use these phrases to position your benefit statements.**

  - This is of critical importance because . . .
  - What this means is . . .
  - I am highlighting this issue because . . .
  - We need to care about this because . . .
  - The key advantage (or benefit) here is . . .
  - If we don't, we stand to lose/gain . . .
  - What is unique (or different) about this benefit is . . .

## STARTING STRONGLY

### Presenting with Impact

> "Look with favor on bold beginnings."
> —VIRGIL

Spend the first 10 to 15 percent of your presentation previewing where you want to go with your presentation. You get just thirty seconds to make a powerful first impression, so it is critical you practice your opening until it is word perfect.

### The Three Functions of an Opening

A dynamic structured opening serves three functions. It has to:

- Grab the audience's attention. The opening must **hook** the audience into listening.

- Provide reasons for listening. This is where you deliver your **positioning statement** and explain to your listeners the benefits of listening—what's in it for them. This is the most critical part of persuasion.

- Describe what you'll talk about. This is where you provide a quick overview or agenda of what you're going to present.

### Churchill's Greatest Opening

As an orator, Winston Churchill has no equal. How did Churchill begin his first speech as prime minister?

> "I have nothing to offer but blood, toil, tears, and sweat."

In May 1940, Churchill was still an unproven leader with a track record of being impetuous and unreliable. His speeches quickly dispelled most reservations.

## HOT TIPS

- **Don't weaken or destroy your opening:**

  - By explaining how you hate presenting in public.
  - By repeating information from the introduction.
  - By starting with, "Before I begin . . ."

- **Tell the audience how long you're planning to talk.** People always appreciate this information.

- **If you're using PowerPoint try using a video clip, evocative visual, or music as a starter.** The net contains a huge range of downloadable, royalty-free material.

- **A three-bullet point agenda works well as an overview.** Audiences especially respect presenters who pay them the courtesy of providing them with direction.

- **Make sure any humorous openings or quotes relate directly to the theme of your presentation.** A story or quote that doesn't quite fit leaves everyone confused and perplexed.

## MAKING YOUR POINT

> "The best way to be boring is to leave nothing out."
>
> —VOLTAIRE

Eighty-to eighty-five percent of the time in a presentation should be spent establishing your case or point of view. Few people can remember more than five points. It takes approximately seven to ten minutes to make a point. That's why experts recommend you don't try to cover more than three points in a thirty-minute presentation.

### Support Each Point with Evidence

The right evidence will clinch your case. Poorly chosen evidence can destroy your presentation. Different people are persuaded by different types of information. Some people like statistics; others prefer anecdotes and quotes.

### Use the Latest Information

Use illustrations, statistics and, expert testimony—the more recent, the better. If your information or statistics are new and surprising, sell that fact.

### Customizing Your Evidence

Its always difficult to judge how much supporting evidence you need to convert a skeptical audience. PowerPoint, however, has a very useful feature where you can hold related groups of backup slides in reserve. This feature allows you to easily customize your presentation to a skeptical audience.

## HOT TIPS

- **Use case studies to support your key points.** Individual case studies are more powerful than statistics.

- **Use novel evidence.** Fresh or repackaged information is more convincing.

- **Cite testimonials from independent third parties.** They're extremely persuasive. Using quotations from highly credible sources increases your credibility.

- **Make your statistics memorable.** Dry statistics are the least memorable type of evidence.

- **Use stories, analogies, and personal experiences.** They humanize your presentation and involve the listener.

- **Add humor.** Liven up your examples with a touch of humor. Tell a joke at your expense. This deepens engagement.

- **Don't try and oversell your case by stretching your point.** You'll simply dilute your argument and cast a shadow over your credibility.

## FINISHING IN STYLE

### End on a Climax

Your conclusion is the last thing people hear. It's your last chance to get through. In a presentation, starting off badly is a setback; finishing badly often signals failure.

> "Great is the art of beginning, but greater is the art of ending."
> —HENRY WORDSWORTH LONGFELLOW

A strong conclusion must:

- **Summarize your presentation.** The conclusion must recap your key points.

- **Provide closure.** The conclusion must end purposefully. Presentations have to "sound finished."

- **Motivate the audience to respond.** You must present a call to action. If your presentation is informative, you may want the audience to reflect on the issues or go away and do research.

### Blood, Sweat, and Tears Ending

Churchill ended his famous 1940 Blood, Sweat, and Tears speech with this call for action:

> "You ask what is our aim? I answer in one word: Victory—victory at all costs. . . . I say, come then, let us go forward together with our united strength."

Is it any wonder Churchill was praised for mobilizing the English language and sending it into battle?

## HOT TIPS

- **Use phrases such as "in conclusion," "finally," or "to conclude"** to signal your ending. People do want to know your speech has ended.

- **Keep your conclusion brief.** It shouldn't take more than 5 to 10 percent of your talk. A long, rambling conclusion can destroy what is potentially a compelling address.

- **Always invite questions.** Announce in your conclusion there will be time for questions. It keeps your audience involved.

- **Leave a memorable last impression.** This is your final chance to influence expectations.

- **Finish with a memorable last line.** End with "I have one final message to leave you with." Then deliver an inspirational point. A spoken ending generally has much more impact than a slide.

- **Don't leave your audience in any doubt as to what you want them to do once the presentation has ended.** They will walk away frustrated and confused.

## BRIDGING WITH TRANSITIONS

### Signposts

Regardless of whether you are presenting a speech or using Power-Point you need to use verbal transition words and statements to your audience. Lead your listeners smoothly from one section or idea to the next. Transitions also provide mini internal summaries that act as signposts to tell the listeners where they are, where they've been, and where they are going.

They also help you hold your audience's attention by tightening your logic, improving retention, and helping you lead them to a climax.

> "The suspense is terrible.
> I hope it will last."
>
> —OSCAR WILDE

### Leading Your Audience

The most important transitions are:

- The transition bridging the introduction and body of your presentation.

- The transitions between your key points.

### Mini Internal Summaries

Internal summaries should be used every time you move from one key point to another. An internal summary should tell your audience what you've just covered and where you're about to move. Announce your transitions and let the audience know you are moving from one point to the next.

If your intention is to persuade, pay particular attention to your transitions. Critics will be looking for flaws in your logic.

### HOT TIPS

- **Reinforce your verbal transitions with non-verbal gestures.** A pause, a change of vocal pitch, or a movement can add dramatic impact to a transition.

- **Memorize your transition statements.** The safest way is to write them on cards. Mark these cards "transition cards" so they signal you are about to change topics.

- **Learn all the common transition words.** Examples include: therefore, furthermore, however, for example, meanwhile, in addition, nevertheless, consequently, moreover, first-second-third, and finally.

- Use a variety of bridging statements. Here are a few of the most useful:

  - To recap . . .
  - For my next point . . .
  - We can now move to . . .
  - In addition . . .
  - Turning to . . .
  - By that I mean . . .
  - In other words . . .

## TRIED AND PROVEN ORGANIZATIONAL PATTERNS

"If you do not know where you are going, every road will get you nowhere."

—HENRY KISSINGER

Facts acquire muscle when they are presented in a way your audience finds easy to understand and retain. Here are four tried and proven patterns.

1. **Sequential/Chronological**
   In a sequential presentation you present events in the sequence they occur (e.g., the steps necessary to diagnose a fault in a computer). A chronological sequence also presents events in the order they occur, but you add dates and times to make it easy and logical for an audience to track.

2. **Topical Order**
   Here you divide your subject into logical segments or subtopics based on your knowledge of the subject.

3. **Physical Location**

This is useful when you want to talk about things that occur at different places or geographical locations.

4. **Contrast and Comparison**
   You can use contrast and comparison when you want your audience to choose between different options or evaluate alternative ideas. The simplest and most common chunking technique is a two-part contrast. The mind readily chunks information into two parts: features/benefits, old/new, issues/actions.

## HOT TIPS

- **When it comes to presenting detailed graphic and sequential information, PowerPoint stands supreme.** Words alone are simply inadequate and can lead to misunderstandings.

- **Summarize step-by-step sequences with a single visual. Flow charts are superb for depicting a series of steps or procedures.**

- **Start with the "big picture"** when you introduce a complex process. Most of your listeners will appreciate an overview before you plunge into the detail.

- **Use acronyms to aid memory.** For example, FUD stands for Fear, Uncertainty, and Doubt.

- **Use a map when you are referring to unknown locations.** Maps are much better than words at communicating distance and scale.

- **When in doubt, use a numbered list.** It is usually the easiest and often the most powerful way to group information.

- **Make sure your information is relevant.** Audiences love information that is relevant and able to be used immediately.

# USE A PERSUASIVE STRUCTURE TO ADD COHERENCE

Your presentation will never come across as a compelling story unless you give it structure and coherence. Here are three of the most useful patterns for persuasive presentations.

## Problem-Solution

The most basic and most potent of all organizational patterns for a persuasive presentation is to create a problem for your audience and then solve it by presenting a convincing solution.

If you are working with an apathetic audience, or your audience seems unaware that a problem exists, then a problem-solution pattern works well. The Motivated Persuasion Sequence shown opposite is a variation of the problem-solving pattern.

## Refutation

Refutation works best as a persuasion strategy when you know your position is under attack or you know what your audience's chief objections to your proposals are.

## Cause and Effect

The cause-and-effect persuasion pattern is similar to the problem-solution pattern. If you want to emphasize the causes, discuss the effect first and then examine the causes. If, by contrast, you wish to highlight the effects of a situation, first present the problem as your central idea and then spell out its effects.

## The Motivated Persuasion Sequence

The motivated sequence is a five-step sequence developed by Alan Monroe. It is based on research on the way we think when we are being persuaded.

1. **Grab your audience's attention.** There are dozens of ways, but you can start with a startling statistic or use humor or anecdote.

2. **Persuade the audience they have a definite need.** Here you have to convince your audience why your topic or case should concern them directly.

3. **Explain how you plan to satisfy the need you've created.** This is your solution.

4. **Now you need to visualize or paint a picture with words on how bright the future will be with your solution.** Alternatively, you could paint a negative visualization and tell your listeners how terrible the future will be if they don't adopt your solution.

5. **Tell the audience what specific action you want them to take.** Don't ever let your audience guess or speculate what you want them to do.

"I was floating in a tunnel toward a very bright light
and then a voice told me I had to go back and
finish listening to the presentation."

# CHAPTER FOUR

# STEP FOUR:
# ADD DRAMA AND IMPACT

• • • • • • • • • • • •

"The object of oratory is not truth, but persuasion."

—LORD MACAULAY

Since most people are moved by a mix of reason and emotion skilled presenters must be able to deliver a presentation that appeals to both head and heart. The PowerPoint presenter who dishes up a diet of word-based slides is simply inviting rejection.

The best PowerPoint presenters like great speakers use emotion grabbing techniques such as stories, quotes, and metaphors to engage their audience. Plus, they use PowerPoint's visual creative capabilities to add additional punch.

## MAKING HEAD AND HEART APPEALS

### Logical and Emotional Appeals

All presentations need support—stories, statistics, and facts—that you use to prove and illustrate your points.

Some people are driven by their heads. When they make a decision they are driven

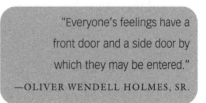

"Everyone's feelings have a front door and a side door by which they may be entered."

—OLIVER WENDELL HOLMES, SR.

by facts, logic, and reason. Others think with their hearts. Emotions are of central importance. Many people are driven by both. They are moved by a mix of reason and emotion.

### Moved by Emotion?

The word emotion comes from the Latin *emovere*. It means to move away or move greatly. As rational human beings we like to think logic drives most decisions. But the fact is, in most persuasive situations people buy on emotion and then justify their decision with fact. People may be persuaded by reason but they are moved by emotion.

### Combine Appeals

The best way to move an audience is to use a mix of emotional and logical appeals. Even hardened analysts respond to emotion, so don't be deterred by those who claim they are only moved by facts.

### Speaking vs. PowerPoint

While PowerPoint excels as a multimedia tool, it is rare to find a PowerPoint slide or even a video clip that can move an audience emotionally the way a gifted speaker can with a story or metaphor.

### HOT TIPS

- **Present your emotional appeal first.** Once we're emotionally receptive, we are much more likely to listen to facts and logic. For emotional pleas to be successful, they must be delivered from the heart.

- **Use a variety of different types of evidence.** Some people like stories and quotes; others prefer statistics and graphical support.

- **Don't weaken your argument by stretching your support.** Even one weak example will undermine your case.

- **Use handouts to avoid data overload.** If your audience is looking for lots of data, tell them you will hand out a summary of all the supporting data after your presentation. One of the great features of PowerPoint is its ability to easily create summary.

- **Use questions to involve your audience.** If you're about to quote data on house sales ask them: "How many of you have purchased a house in the past two years?"

- **Plan for long-term retention.** People forget 80 percent of what they hear in four days.

## TAPPING INTO THE POWER OF STORIES

Stories bring presentations alive. Most great persuaders use stories to drive their message home. Socrates and Homer

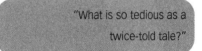
"What is so tedious as a twice-told tale?"

taught with stories. Jesus spoke in parables. Lincoln, Churchill and Kennedy used anecdotes to make many of their most telling points. The best PowerPoint presentations I've seen have been laced with

tention. Like a movie, stories have a he audience to relate to.

ideas and make abstract concepts

ner's emotions better than dry sets

. A vivid story stays in the listener's mind long after everything else is forgotten.

### What's the Purpose?

A story must have a purpose. The first question you must ask when reading a story is, what is the purpose? What is the lesson, moral, or punchline of this story? One of the quickest ways to ruin a presentation is to tell a pointless story.

## HOT TIPS

- **Tell personal stories.** The audience *will* want to share your experience. Remember, you are the expert.

- **Tell stories about people.** Stories with real or imaginary characters humanize a presentation.

- **Summarize the lesson.** Stories can have more than one lesson.

- **Start with short stories.** Build your confidence up with short stories thirty seconds to one minute long. A 150-word story takes about one minute of speech time.

- **Test your stories before delivery.** A colleague or friend will tell you if you need, for example, to reduce or increase detail—both common faults.

- **Beware of overused stories.** They damage your reputation.

- **Start a story file.** Collect all your favorite stories and file them under different topics or themes.

## QUOTING FOR IMPACT

### Memorable Sound Bites

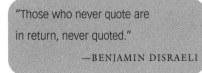

"Those who never quote are in return, never quoted."

—BENJAMIN DISRAELI

"I often quote myself, it adds spice to the conversation," said British playwright George Bernard Shaw. Most of us, however, lack Shaw's talents to invent compelling, interesting sound bites.

## Pithy and Profound

"Great speeches always have great sound bites . . . They sum up a point or make a point that is pithy and profound," says presidential speechwriter Peggy Noonan.

If someone has said something on your topic that is more authoritative, compelling or interesting than what you can say—and can be delivered as a soundbite—use it.

## Stick to the Point

Quotes must always make a point. Irrelevant quotes weaken your impact, especially when they come across as a crude form of "name dropping."

## Use Fresh Sources

Try and find quotes which are fresh or offbeat. If you are going to quote a favorite from Lincoln, Churchill or Martin Luther King, come up with a fresh angle. Audiences love new information about an old favorite.

## The C-R-E-A-M Acronym

Presidential speechwriter James C. Humes uses the acronym **CREAM** to spell the five different ways great presenters create quotes.

**C**ontrast

*"With malice toward none, with charity for all . . ."*
Abraham Lincoln

**R**hyme

*"Let us have faith that right makes might . . ."*
Abraham Lincoln

**E**cho
*"Never in the field of human conflict was so much owed by so many to so few."*
Winston Churchill

**A**lliteration

People *"will not be judged by the color of their skin, but by the content of their character."*
Martin Luther King

**M**etaphor
*"From Stettin in the Baltic to Trieste in the Adriatic, an iron curtain has descended across the continent."*
Winston Churchill

# PERSUADING WITH METAPHORS AND ANALOGIES

### The Power of Metaphors

A metaphor is an imaginative way of describing something by saying it is something else. Metaphors are powerful because they allow us to personify abstract

> "Metaphors are much more tenacious than facts."
>
> —PAUL DE MAN

ideas. In general, they are more powerful and persuasive than facts or statistics, or even the most sizzling PowerPoint graphics.

### Churchill and Lady Astor

Churchill loved using zoological metaphors to attack his opponents. He once ridiculed Lady Astor and her pro-German supporters in Parliament, saying, "An appeaser is one who feeds the crocodile hoping it will eat him last."

The attack so upset Nancy Astor that when she met Churchill at a dinner party she said, "Winston, if I were your wife, I'd put poison in your coffee." In a flash, Churchill countered, "And if I were your husband, Nancy, I'd drink it."

### The Power of Analogies

Analogies can have the same impact as metaphors. An analogy allows you to introduce a new idea quickly by comparing it with something familiar and simple.

When Benjamin Franklin said, "Fish and visitors start to smell in three days," he was delivering a vivid message of why we tire of visitors who wear out their welcome.

## HOT TIPS

- **Use metaphors and analogies to simplify complex concepts.** By comparing the complex and abstract with something simple and concrete, your listeners understand by association.

- **Use metaphors to reframe the way your audience thinks.** Franklin Roosevelt, when calling for support to provide lend-lease aid to Great Britain in 1940, said, "Who of you, if you saw your neighbor's house on fire, would not lend him your hose to put out the fire?"

- **Test your metaphors for comprehensiveness. When selecting a metaphor ask:**

  - What does my metaphor highlight?
  - What does my metaphor conceal?
  - What does my metaphor distort?

- **Analyze your audience's metaphors before you present.** Most groups share common metaphors or mindsets that shape their thinking and attitudes.

## USING STATISTICS

### Lies, Damned Lies

> "Torture the statistics long enough and they'll confess to anything."
>
> —T-SHIRT SLOGAN

British Prime Minister Benjamin Disraeli said there are "three kinds of lies: lies, damned lies and statistics." Nevertheless, we can't avoid the fact that statistics are often portrayed as the ultimate in hard evidence.

### Use Credible Sources

Statisticians say "figures don't lie but liars figure." And since skeptics know that figures can be used to support any argument, make your statistics credible by citing authoritative, unbiased sources.

### Make Your Numbers Understandable

Large numbers are especially difficult to understand. Few of us, for example, can intuitively grasp the difference between one million and one billion.

If you want someone to grasp the relative magnitude of a million and a billion, you might say that it takes only eleven-and-a-half days for a million seconds to pass, whereas it takes thirty-two years for a billion seconds to pass.

## Use Comparisons

To highlight the speed of the supersonic Concorde, you might say, "The Concorde's velocity is 400,000 times that of a snail."

## HOT TIPS

- **Don't use loaded phrases. To emphasise a large number say:**

  - More than two-thirds
  - Nearly seven out of ten
  - More than two out of three

- **To play down a figure say:**

  - Less than three-quarters
  - Fewer than two out of three
  - Under two-thirds

- **Round off numbers to improve recall.** It is much easier to visualize and remember three million than 3,168,758. About 30 percent is easier to remember than 31.69 percent.

- **Personalize your statistics.** Imagine starting a speech on our sexual habits like this: "Of the half of us who have pets at home, 45.5 percent allow them in the room during sex."

- **Don't use loaded phrases.** Value-laden comments such as "an incredible two-thirds" and "amazing 70 percent" create suspicion.

## THE POWER OF THREE

A remarkably common organisational pattern in successful presentations is the "rule of threes." Although we don't fully understand the psychological reasons behind the role of threes, information is extraordinarily compelling when it is clustered in groups of three: three points, three arguments, three phrases.

### Memorable Examples

- The Trinity—"Father, Son and Holy Ghost."

- Julius Caesar—"I came, I saw, I conquered."

- Robert the Bruce—"Try, try and try again."

- Franklin D. Roosevelt—"I see one-third of a nation ill-housed, ill-clad, ill-nourished."

- Abraham Lincoln—"Of the people, by the people, for the people."

- Danton—"To dare, to dare again, ever to dare."

### Mundane Examples

On a more mundane level we talk about the three-beat conservation slogan (reduce, reuse, recycle), the three-step commands, (ready, aim, fire), and the three Rs of education (reading, writing and 'rithmetic). Then there are the Three Bears, the Three Stooges and the Three Little Pigs.

### HOT TIPS

- **Vary your three-part lists.**

  - **Consider three words:**
    *"Never, never, never give up."*
    WINSTON CHURCHILL

- **Consider three phrases:**
  *"Government of the people, for the people, by the people."*
  ABRAHAM LINCOLN

- **Consider three sentences:**
  *"Dogs look up to us.*
  *Cats look down on us.*
  *Pigs treat us as equals."*
  WINSTON CHURCHILL

- **Make the last item in your list your most important.** Then give it added weight by making it longer.
  *"The inalienable right to life, liberty and the pursuit of happiness."*
  AMERICAN DECLARATION OF INDEPENDENCE

- **Slow down and pause when you present your three-part lists.** You'll lose all the impact of a three-part phrase if you rush through.

## PERSUADING WITH VISUALS

### Visuals Increase Persuasion

Great visuals are attention grabbers. They make a huge difference to a successful PowerPoint presentation. Seventy-five percent of what we learn comes to us visually, 13 percent through hearing, and 12 per-

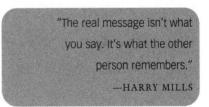
"The real message isn't what you say. It's what the other person remembers."
—HARRY MILLS

cent through smell, taste, and touch. A study by the University of Minnesota and 3M found that the presenters who use visuals are 43 percent more persuasive than those who don't.

### Visuals Have Staying Power

Visuals increase retention. Listeners may forget a speaker's words within minutes of leaving a presentation. But they can remember a picture—in detail—weeks later.

### Visuals Simplify Concepts

Visuals make information easy to digest. The mind stores and processes information in pictures. If you cannot picture an idea before you present it, you're unlikely to communicate it successfully.

### PowerPoint is a Primarily Visual Tool

PowerPoint's potency comes from its ability to create and deliver visuals. Presenters who turn their slideshows into bullet data dumps deserve tar and feathering.

## HOT TIPS

- **Determine your message first.** The prime purpose is to communicate a persuasive message, not to dazzle with graphic effects.

- **Think K.I.S.S. (Keep It Short and Simple).** With visuals less is more.

- **One thought per visual.** Organize all visuals around one specific point.

- **Test all visuals for visibility.** They must be viewable from the back of the room.

- **Give every visual a headline.** It should be simple, brief, and communicate the purpose of the visual.

- **Organize your content around three to five points.** Most audiences struggle to remember more than five key points.

- **Don't present more than one slide every two minutes.** A twenty-minute presentation should, therefore, contain no more than ten slides.

## THE POTENCY OF VISUALS

Tony Buzan, in his book *Mindmapping*, argues: "Color, line, dimension, textures, visual rhythm, and especially imagination . . .

Images are . . . more evocative than words, more precise and potent in triggering a wide range of associations, thereby enhancing creativity and memory."

## The Speed of Perception

Former Saatchi and Saatchi Creative Director, Michael Newman, tells us: "The human brain interprets an image infinitely faster than it deciphers words, which have to travel through various other cerebral regions before their meaning can be constructed.

A visual image falling on the retina, for example, takes about a quarter of a second to flash into our conscious perception. Before it gets there, each of the components of the image—color, shape, movement, and location—has to be identified separately by various specialized parts of the brain.

These components are assembled into a pattern that is then sent onward to regions that try to attach some meaning to it."

Seneca said, "Arguments are like eels: However logical, they may slip from the mind's weak grasp unless fixed there by imagery and style. We need metaphors to derive a sense of what cannot be seen or touched, or else we will forget."

The message is clear. Whenever you need to change perceptions, first consider visuals.

"Bagley's presentation wasn't so bad. Sometime during the third hour, my spirit left my body and went to the beach!"

# CHAPTER FIVE

# STEP FIVE:
# REHEARSE UNTIL PERFECT

• • • • • • • • • • • •

*"It usually takes more than three weeks to prepare a good impromptu speech."*

—MARK TWAIN

I've never yet rehearsed for a speech or a PowerPoint presentation without having to make changes. Audiences admire, listen to, and are influenced by presenters who respect them and their time by rehearsing until they are word, picture, and time perfect.

## SPEAKING WITH NOTES

There are three ways to give a speech:

> *"First he read his speech, second he read it badly, third it wasn't worth reading."*
>
> —WINSTON CHURCHILL

- You can memorize it by heart.

- You can read it from a typed script.

- You can speak extemporaneously using notes as a guide.

### Memorization

Memorizing a speech by heart and delivering it is very hard for beginners. My advice is not to try. Some professional speakers can do it because they often reuse the same speech on multiple audiences. Churchill would never deliver an important speech without carefully organized and edited notes.

### Reading

Reading a speech presents its own unique problems. We cover these on the page opposite.

### Speaking with Notes

For most speakers notes insure against memory loss, and you can change course if you need to. And more importantly, notes allow you to make eye contact and speak in a conversational style while still holding your structure.

### Use a Numbered Outline

Some speakers seem to think notes are an excuse to abandon their structure. Use a numbered outline to create a skeleton and a map. When you glance down at your notes, you always need to know where you are.

## HOT TIPS

- **For a speech, use index cards to take notes.** Use one side of the card only and don't overload it.

- **Use key words and key phrases** rather than complete sentences for the bulk of a speech. Whole sentences encourage you to read from the notes like a script.

- **Write out the first and last sentences in full.** Writing the first sentence removes the fear of a mental block. Writing the last sentence ensures a smooth, professional ending.

- **Write out statistics, direct quotations, and key transitions in full.** You can't afford to get these wrong.

- **As you finish with each card, cut it from the deck.** Put it in your pocket or somewhere else. Then if you drop or mix up your deck, you don't have to sort out the discards.

- **Notes are not a sign of weakness.** They show you respect the audience and the occasion enough to put time into preparation.

## READING A SPEECH FROM A SCRIPT

### To Read or Not to Read

Reading a speech can be a perilous experience. We've all cringed as we've watched speakers read their speeches in a mechanical, monotonous, wooden way.

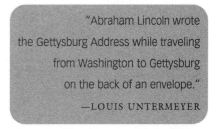

"Abraham Lincoln wrote the Gettysburg Address while traveling from Washington to Gettysburg on the back of an envelope."

—LOUIS UNTERMEYER

### The Two Biggest Mistakes

When amateurs read a speech they often make two big mistakes:

- Their delivery and pacing sounds stilted and unnatural.

- They quickly lose eye contact with their audience.

### The Churchill Formula

The unnatural delivery is caused by the speaker trying to memorize blocks of sentences. The lack of eye contact is caused by the speaker talking while his eyes are looking down at his script.

The trick is, as Churchill discovered, to memorize a sound bite of words, bring your head up, pause, and then deliver your sound bite. Churchill perfected the technique. So until Churchill was praised as the greatest orator of the twentieth century, Ronald Reagan used the same technique.

### Type for Easy Reading

Have your speech typed out for easy reading. Type it in a teleprompter format, like the Gettysburg example that follows.

## Reading Gettysburg

The introduction to Lincoln's famous Gettysburg Address has been set out below. It is laid out to be read thought by thought. It has also been spaced for easy reading. I've also underlined the words that need additional vocal emphasis.

**Four** score and **seven** years ago

**our** fathers

brought forth upon **this** continent

a **new** nation

conceived in **liberty,**

and dedicated to the proposition that

**all** men are created equal.

**Now** we are engaged in a **great** civil war,

**testing** whether **that** nation,

or **any** nation

**so** conceived and **so** dedicated

can long **endure.**

## USING SPEAKER NOTES AS HANDOUTS IN POWERPOINT

In general, I prefer to distribute handouts at the end so I can keep the audience focused on the slideshow. There is nothing worse than having an audience member scan through your handout and then sit back, seemingly disinterested in what you are about to present.

> "I read part of it all the way through."
>
> —SAM GOLDWYN
> AMERICAN MOTION
> PICTURE DIRECTOR

### Speaker Notes

PowerPoint lets you type your speaker notes into a large text box which sits under or besides a picture of your slide. The thing to remember with PowerPoint is you are not just using the speaker notes to keep track of your spoken words.

PowerPoint has a number of features, such as text builds and transitions, that are dependent on good presenter management and timing for maximum impact. Your speaker notes are where you keep all your reminders about when to emphasize a particular point or insert an additional slide.

### Handouts

With PowerPoint you can create handouts in a variety of formats. The format of the handout will depend on the purpose of your presentation and the content of your slides.

If your presentation slides are primarily visual you might want to give your audience a handout of your slides at the beginning so they can add notes as you speak. If your presentation is controversial or has an element of surprise, then wait for the completion of your presentation to provide your handouts.

### HOT TIPS

- **Use your speaker notes to highlight the added value points you want to add to what is already on the slide.** Never insult your audience by just reading out what is already on the slide.

- **Jot your key points down as short bullet points.** They're easier to scan than full sentences plus you can't be tempted to read them out word for word.

- **Write out any technical reminder in a different color to your spoken context.**

- **Break all the material you have to read or quote into sound bite form.** Space it out and underline the key words as shown in the Gettysburg address example on page 64.

- **Keep your handouts brief, highly visual, and succinct.** Handouts should never act as substitutes for written reports.

## PRACTICING FOR PERFECTION

> "Doing the common things uncommonly well."
>
> —ORISON SWETT MARDEN

Arthur Rubenstein, the great pianist, liked to say: "If I don't practice for one day, I know it; if I don't practice for two days, my critics know it; and if I miss three days—the audience knows it."

After delivering two thousand performances of *Othello*, the master Shakespearean actor Sir Lawrence Olivier continued to practice.

### Start Early

Practice until you're supremely confident. You can't over-practice. Every time you practice you'll find something to improve. Don't listen to those who say you'll lose your spontaneity if you rehearse. Last-minute practice creates its own unneeded pressures. So finish drafting your presentation at least two days before you have to perform.

### Rehearse Out Loud

You must rehearse out loud. Silent practice never works. When you rehearse in silence you never make a mistake.

### Seek Feedback

After two or three practice sessions alone, ask a friend or colleague for feedback. Start with the problem parts, then finish with a full dress rehearsal.

## HOT TIPS

- **Videotape your address.** It's the best way to observe your vocal and physical mannerisms and your use of technology. Ask yourself:

  - Do I look confident and enthusiastic?

  - Am I speaking too slowly or too fast?

  - Do I need to eliminate any irritating non-verbal mannerisms?

  - Do I sound conversational?

  - Do sections need to be reworded?

  - Do I interact seamlessly with the technology?

- **Time your presentations** to make sure your presentation is the right length.

- **During rehearsals time each major part.** Then you can judge where to make cuts if you have to.

- **Don't practice in front of a mirror.** Looking at yourself while practicing is artificial and a huge distraction.

- **Stand up.** Always practice standing up so you can practice your gestures as well as your words.

"I suffer from corporate insomnia. I have trouble falling asleep during dull business presentations."

# CHAPTER SIX

# STEP SIX:
# DELIVER WITH STYLE

. . . . . . . . . . . . .

*"Preach not because you have to say something, but because you have something to say."*

—RICHARD WHATELY

They way you present and the way you talk is at least as important as what you present. Remember, presenting is a performing art. No one will believe an upbeat positive message that is delivered by an inert, monotone speaker who looks and acts nervous and comes across as an inept drone.

## OVERCOMING STAGE FRIGHT

### Presentation Panic

Stage fright is extraordinarily common. According to one survey, most people rate public speaking more frightening than death.

> *"Stage fright is the sweat of perfection."*
> —EDWARD R. MURROW

Abraham Lincoln suffered from stage fright; so too did Sir Lawrence Olivier and countless other celebrities. The key is learn to manage it and turn it to your advantage.

### The Instant Calming Sequence (ICS)

There are dozens of effective stress management techniques. One of the best is the Instant Calming Sequence (ICS) popularized by Robert K. Cooper Ph.D. Based on techniques developed by martial arts exponents, ICS gives you inner control of your mind, emotions, and body whenever you feel nervous.

Because ICS is performed while you are fully alert with your eyes wide open, you can use it virtually anywhere.

### Step 1: Breathe Smoothly

Under stress, most of us halt our breathing for a few seconds, reducing our oxygen intake to the brain, thereby creating increased anxiety and tension. The ICS command, breathe smoothly, helps you establish control.

### Step 2: Smile

Research shows a smile, even when you don't feel like smiling, increases the flow of blood to the brain, protecting your nervous system from negative stress. So, learning to smile in moments of stress can be an uplifting skill in times of challenge.

### Step 3: Maintain an Upright Posture

Slouching, tightening, or collapsing your chest magnifies negative feelings. Slouching can reduce blood flow and oxygen intake, thereby slowing down reaction time. Your posture typically mirrors or reflects the way you feel. So consciously engaging in an upright posture works wonders.

### Step 4: Sweep Away Tension

Scanning your muscles and sending out a mental signal to relax allows you to locate the source of tension and clears away anxiety. When we are under stress, we tighten up, and our energy levels drop along with reaction speeds.

## The Instant Calming Sequence

1. **Breathe smoothly, deeply and evenly.** Deep breathing relaxes and calms you down.

2. **Smile.** A smile makes your body less reactive to negative stress.

3. **Maintain an upright posture.** Don't let your body tense or slump even slightly.

4. **Sweep away tension.** Scan your body in one fast sweep of the mind—from your scalp to your toes—to locate any tension. Simultaneously flash a mental wave of relaxation across your mind, as if you are standing under a waterfall that washes away all excess tension.

5. **Face reality.** Focus and concentrate intently on the problem in a calm, clear, focused manner.

### Step 5: Face Reality

To avoid mental paralysis, you must acknowledge reality and learn to face it calmly and clearly.

Presenters who know how to handle stress don't worry about things they can't control. They focus on their own behaviors. What could potentially be negative stress can be transformed into a motivating and engaging experience.

# USE HIGH-IMPACT BODY TALK

> "The body says what words cannot."
> —MARTHA GRAHAM

Professional presenters often claim body talk can be measured precisely. They cite the figures of UCLA professor Albert Mehrebian:

- 55 percent of the message impact is communicated to us visually (body language).

- 38 percent is communicated vocally (tone of voice).

- Just 7 percent is communicated verbally (spoken words).

## The 93 Percent–7 Percent Split

Mehrebian's figures suggest the spoken words account for just 7 percent of the impact and the nonverbal component accounts for 93 percent of a speaker's message.

However, Mehrebian's figures are exaggerated. In presentations where the content is important the words are just as important as the nonverbal message. Nevertheless, in most presentations where your body talk and words clash, your audience will rely on the body talk for their message.

## Posture Don'ts

- Don't lean on the podium.

- Don't put your hands on your hips.

- Don't fold your arms.

- Don't sway.

- Don't fold your arms.

- Don't clasp your hands behind your back.

- Don't stand in the fig leaf position.

# The S-O-F-T-E-N Body Talk Formula

Remember the acronym *SOFTEN* when you stand up to deliver a speech.

**Smile:** Smile to generate warmth.

**Open stance:** Stand with an open posture with your legs apart and arms ready to gesture.

**Forward lean:** Move your weight forward onto the balls of your feet.

**Tone:** Vary your voice pitch, rate, and rhythm.

**Eye contact:** Make eye contact with all sections of the audience.

**Nod:** Punctuate your speech with nods and purposeful gestures.

## POWER WORDS

### Words Evoke Emotions

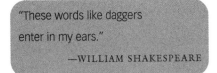

"These words like daggers enter in my ears."

—WILLIAM SHAKESPEARE

Top presenters choose their words with great precision. The right words can move people to agreement. The wrong words can result in deadlock and animosity.

### Warm and Cold Words

There are warm words and cold words just as there are warm and cold colors. Warm words help us feel safe and secure. Cold words create doubt and unease. Cold words have their place but use them with care.

| WARM WORDS | COLD WORDS |
|---|---|
| Agree | Abnormal |
| Approval | Afraid |
| Basic | Cannot |
| Care | Disagree |
| Fair | Disappoint |
| Fresh | Fruitless |
| Fun | Nonsense |
| Good | Ruthless |
| Hope | Underhand |
| Independent | Unfair |
| New | Unfortunately |
| Sincere | Warning |

## Words That Sell

Here is a list of some of the most persuasive words in the English language. Use them to persuade and convince and present your case.

| | |
|---|---|
| Improve | Gain |
| Reduce | Discovery |
| Quick | Genuine |
| Results | Easy |
| Effortless | Clear |
| Save | You |
| Increase | Guarantee |
| Proven | Money |
| Convenient | Authentic |
| Have | Safe |
| Thorough | Respected |
| New | Unique |
| Original | Positive |
| Love | Memorable |
| Promise | Reliable |
| Yes | Tested |

The most persuasive word of all these words is **new.**

# USING ASSERTIVE LANGUAGE

## Be Congruent

> "Sticks and stones can break your bones, but words can make your blood boil."
>
> —CULLEN HIGHTOWER

If your body language and voice are congruent, the other party will listen to your words. If your words clash with your body talk, people will believe your body talk.

Effective presenters use assertive rather than aggressive or passive language to state clearly what they want, feel, and think. Powerful speakers also eliminate words that weaken the language.

## Communicate Strength

Assertive speakers choose words that convey strength and authority. Assertive speakers put themselves forward without ever putting the other person down. They speak clearly, directly, and use lots of "I" phrases.

| ASSERTIVE WORDS | WEAK WORDS |
| --- | --- |
| I require | I would like |
| I need | I wish |
| I want | I hope |
| I must | I prefer |

## HOT TIPS

- **Use strong words.** If you feel strongly about something, use words to match. *"This is the best way"* is much better than *"I think this is the best way."*

- **Leave out intensifiers.** Intensifiers like *very, definitely,* and *surely* do the opposite of what they are supposed to do.

- **Avoid fillers.** Powerless speakers hesitate a lot and rely on fillers like "uh," "umm," and "well."

- **Don't be overly polite.** Powerless speakers use "please" and "thank you" excessively. Over-politeness conveys timidity and uncertainty.

- **Avoid weak statements such as:**

  - You may not agree with me, but . . .
  - This may not be what you're thinking, however . . .
  - I'm not 100 percent certain, but . . .

- **Match your body talk to your words.** Use the SOFTEN formula to align your body talk with your message.

## DEVELOP VOCAL IMPACT

### Commanding Voice

Few of the great silent film stars survived the arrival of the talking movies in 1927. They simply lacked verbal impact. Even the great Rudolph Valentino couldn't overcome his small, squeaky voice.

> "He speaks to me as if I were a public meeting."
> —QUEEN VICTORIA

### Your Voice Is Your Calling Card

If you sound energetic and confident, very likely you will be viewed as energetic and confident. If you sound weak and timid, you will probably be seen as weak and timid.

If you sound shrill and strident, people will probably treat you accordingly. Your voice can reveal how relaxed or tense you are, how tired you are, and can even indicate your emotional state.

### The Ideal Pace

Most speakers average 120 to 180 words a minute. There is no ideal speed. The best rate depends upon your style as a speaker and your message.

Great speakers' rates of delivery vary greatly. Franklin Roosevelt spoke at 110 words a minute; President Kennedy raced along at 180 words a minute. Martin Luther King Jr. began his "I have a dream" speech at 92 words a minute and finished at 145.

## HOT TIPS

- **Vary your pace to generate interest.** If you speak slowly, consciously speed up from time to time. If you speak fast, consciously slow right down.

- **Use a low pitch to project authority.** A lower pitch is interpreted as authoritative and influential.

- **Control the loudness.** Vary your volume by stressing the most important words and phrases.

- **Whisper for impact.** If you are naturally a loud and forceful speaker, dropping down to a near whisper can be very powerful.

- **Sharpen your articulation.** Clear, crisp words convey confidence and competence.

- **Master pauses for impact.** As Mark Twain said, "There is nothing so powerful as the rightly timed pause." Persuasive speakers use pauses for emphasis, effect, and mood.

- **Use rhetorical questions to increase vocal impact.** Your voice will automatically rise as you ask them.

## STAYING CENTER STAGE

### PowerPoint is a Speaker Support Tool

Never forget that PowerPoint, for all its potency, is nothing more than a speaker support tool. No matter how great your graphics you the speaker must remain center stage.

PowerPoint is there to support you, not the other way around. Working with a laptop, a data projector, and a screen presents several challenges.

## Four Killer Errors

**Error One:** It's very easy to lose eye contact with your audience by spending too much time looking at your laptop or screen.

**Error Two:** It's easy to stand in the wrong place placing yourself between your audience and the screen.

**Error Three:** It's very easy for your presentation to falter as you struggle to master the technology.

**Error Four:** Worst of all, presenters let the PowerPoint drive the presentation by reading each slide word for word.

## HOT TIPS

- **Speak to the audience not to the screen.** You must make eye contact with each person in your audience.

- **Stand where everyone can see you.** If unsure, ask the audience, "Do I need to move back so you can see?"

- **Don't read your text points out loud.** Add value by adding insights or tell an engaging story about a slide.

- **Keep the arrow of the point still on the screen.** A shaky arrow suggests you are nervous.

- **Do two rehearsals.** Do a full dress rehearsal a week before your speech. Then do a mini-rehearsal on the day of your presentation.

- **Stand where you can see the audience, screen, and notes.** Where you stand will vary according to the room setup and size of screen.

# HANDLING TOUGH AND TRICKY QUESTIONS

## Welcome Questions

"There aren't any embarrassing questions—just embarrassing answers."

—CARL ROWAN

Whenever possible, end your talk with a question-and-answer session. Questions increase interaction, commitment, and persuasion.

## Why Don't People Ask Questions?

If your audience doesn't ask questions:

- They don't understand what you've said.

- They fear a question will make them look stupid.

- They switched off during your presentation.

- They want to leave.

- They may feel intimidated by your presence or style of presentation.

## Keep Control

Some speakers are terrified they will lose control in the question-and-answer session. Start by setting out the ground rules. Begin by limiting the types of questions you'll have time for. Say, "I have ten minutes available for questions and I'm happy to deal with any questions on . . . (specify topic)."

## Practice

Practice your question-and-answer session. Anticipate the likely tough questions and practice answering them.

## HOT TIPS

- **Always look the listener in the eye.** Then answer the question briefly and confidently.

- **Announce early when and how you will answer questions.** Ask people to hold their questions until the end of a session.

- **Don't say "that's a good question."** When you compliment one questioner, you are implicitly downgrading the other questions.

- **If you don't know the answer, admit it.** Say, "I'm sorry, I don't have that information." If possible, promise to find out and get back to them.

- **Deflect loaded questions.** Use a bridging statement to keep control such as:

  - "Let's look at it from a broader perspective . . ."
  - "There is an equally important concern . . ."
  - "Let's not lose sight of the underlying problem . . ."

- **Beware of hypothetical questions.** They're usually designed to entrap.

GLASBERGEN

"I'm a very popular business speaker. I can talk for 90 minutes
without actually saying anything. That way, nobody feels guilty
or ashamed for not paying attention and that's good for morale."

# CHAPTER SEVEN

# STEP SEVEN: REVIEW AND REVISE

• • • • • • • • • • • • • •

"I do not object to people looking at their watches when I am speaking.
But I strongly object when they start shaking them to make sure they are still going."

—LORD WILLIAM NORMAN BIRKETT

Top presenters brutally critique every presentation they deliver.
They know presentation is a performing act, which requires continual review and ongoing practice.

## EVALUATE YOUR PERFORMANCE

Use the evaluation form to pinpoint your strengths and weaknesses. Give it to a colleague or friend who you know will give you honest feedback. Don't try to fix everything at once. Pick one or two items to work on each time.

| Presenter Evaluation | | | |
|---|---|---|---|
| **Presenter:** <br> **Evaluator:** | | | |
| Use the following scale: | | | |
| 1 = Yes | 2 = Needs Attention | | 3 = No |
| **Audience** | | | |
| Tailored to audience | 1 | 2 | 3 |
| Clear purpose | 1 | 2 | 3 |
| Achieved purpose | 1 | 2 | 3 |
| Purpose appropriate for audience | 1 | 2 | 3 |
| **Introduction** | | | |
| Confident speaker | 1 | 2 | 3 |
| Grabbed listener's attention | 1 | 2 | 3 |
| Established need to listen | 1 | 2 | 3 |
| Provided overview | 1 | 2 | 3 |
| **Body** | | | |
| Easy to follow | 1 | 2 | 3 |
| Clear transitions | 1 | 2 | 3 |
| Compelling evidence | 1 | 2 | 3 |
| Clear memorable points | 1 | 2 | 3 |
| Vivid support (stories, etc.) | 1 | 2 | 3 |
| Persuasive language | 1 | 2 | 3 |
| Established credibility | 1 | 2 | 3 |
| High impact visuals | 1 | 2 | 3 |

| Conclusion | | | |
|---|---|---|---|
| Summarized key points | 1 | 2 | 3 |
| Memorable conclusion | 1 | 2 | 3 |
| Called for action | 1 | 2 | 3 |
| Handled questions | 1 | 2 | 3 |
| **Body Language** | | | |
| Good eye contact | 1 | 2 | 3 |
| Appropriate gestures | 1 | 2 | 3 |
| Strong confident posture | 1 | 2 | 3 |
| Professional appearance | 1 | 2 | 3 |
| **Voice** | | | |
| Right pace | 1 | 2 | 3 |
| Clear articulation | 1 | 2 | 3 |
| Correct pronunciation | 1 | 2 | 3 |
| Clearly audible | 1 | 2 | 3 |
| Varied pitch | 1 | 2 | 3 |
| Effective pauses | 1 | 2 | 3 |
| **PowerPoint** | | | |
| Confident with technology | 1 | 2 | 3 |
| Compelling storyline | 1 | 2 | 3 |
| Logical structure | 1 | 2 | 3 |
| Persuasive visuals | 1 | 2 | 3 |

PART TWO

POWERPOINT MAGIC:

HOW TO DESIGN AND

DELIVER PERSUASIVE

POWER POINTS

PowerPoint can be a highly potent presentation tool if it is used well.

First, presenters always need to focus on how the mind processes multimedia messages. Our working memories can only handle a limited amount of information at any one time. The biggest mistake presenters make is to present too much information too fast.

Second, presenters need to remind themselves that PowerPoint is primarily a visual tool. PowerPoint's impact comes from its ability to display persuasive visuals.

Finally, presenters need to guard against text overload. Power points that consist of endless text are presentation killers.

"My PowerPoint presentation went so well,
I had it made into a tattoo!"

# CHAPTER EIGHT

# PERSUASION STRATEGIES: HOW TO OPTIMIZE THE PERSUASIVE IMPACT OF POWERPOINT

. . . . . . . . . . . . .

"Take time to deliberate; but when the time for action arrives, stop thinking and go in."

—ANDREW JACKSON

Too often presenters forget that their audience consists of humans whose limited brains impose severe limitations on how much information they can digest and retain.

Here are six high-impact PowerPoint persuasion strategies:

## STRATEGY 1. ALIGN POWERPOINT WITH THE WAY THE BRAIN WORKS

### How the Mind Works

PowerPoint is a multimedia tool that presents words and pictures. To understand how to optimize PowerPoint, we need to know how the mind responds to, processes, and retains multimedia messages.

> "The mind is like the stomach. It is not how much you put into it that counts, but how much it digests."
>
> —A. J. NOCK

### One Mind, Two Channels

Cognitive scientists such as Richard Mayer tell us the brain has two channels for processing information. The visual channel processes information that transmits through the eyes such as diagrams, animation, video, and on-screen text. The verbal channel processes information that comes through the ears such as speech and non-verbal sounds.

### Limited Capacity

The problem for PowerPoint presenters is that our working memory can only grasp a limited amount of words and pictures at any one time. So when a presenter presents images, we can only hold a few images in our working memory. And when a presenter speaks, we can only hold a few words at a time.

### Active Processing

Finally, we don't understand what is being presented until we actively process what we are seeing and hearing by selecting, organizing, and integrating the information.

## One Mind, Two Channels

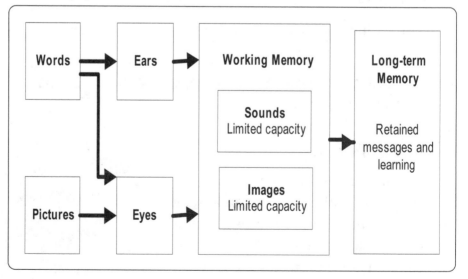

To take advantage of how the mind processes multimedia information, ask:

1. Does your presentation use both channels by presenting related and complementary information in both words and pictures?

2. Does your presentation avoid information overload by optimizing the limited capacity of both processing channels?

3. Does your presentation encourage active processing by giving our viewers the opportunity to select, organize, and integrate presented information?*

## STRATEGY 2. SEGMENT YOUR STORY INTO VISUALLY DIGESTIBLE BITES

### Too Much, Too Fast

Much of the brain overload caused by PowerPoint comes from presenters who present too much, too fast. No wonder so many PowerPoint watchers suffer from *MEGO* (**M**ine **E**yes **G**laze **O**ver) syndrome.

> "Knowledge is a process of piling up facts; wisdom lies in their simplification."
> —MARTIN H. FISCHER

### Use the Billboard Test

Viewers absorb information when it is presented as scannable, bite-sized chunks. So limit your slides to just one point.

A viewer should be able to scan and digest the core content of your slide in less than ten seconds. Think of your slide as a billboard. Billboard designers know they have, at best, a few seconds to catch

*This section owes its structure and many of the insights to Richard Mayer's research. See: Mayer, R.E. *Multimedia Learning*, Cambridge University Press, 2001; Mayer, R.E. & R Moreno, "Nine Ways to Reduce Cognitive Load in Multimedia Learning," *Educational Psychologist*, 38 (1), 43–52; Cliff Atkinson and Richard E Mayer, (2004), "Five Ways to Reduce PowerPoint Overload," www.sociablemedia.com.

a driver's attention so they deliberately keep the message punchy, lean, and sharp.

## Pace Your Presentation

High-speed presentations rarely convince. A few slides presented slowly at a calm, measured pace with plenty of time for audience interaction usually works best.

Remember whatever you do, your audience will forget over 80 percent of what you present within twenty-four hours. So your task is to focus in on the 20 percent of critical content they need to remember.

## HOT TIPS

- **Present no more than ten slides in thirty minutes.** This will make you trim your slide content down to its essential minimum, plus allow ample time for discussion.

- **Transfer the information you reluctantly cut out of your presentation into your handout.** A handout should be much more than a paper copy of your slides. A slideshow illustrating the main features of PowerPoint 2007 might be fifteen slides. The associated handout, which elaborates the features, might well be twenty-five pages with 2,000 words of additional text.

- **Use the slide sorter to continually assess the visual impact of your complete slideshow.** If it looks visually daunting, it needs to be leaned down.

- **If you can't summarize the point of any slide in a single sound bite, break the offending slide into two.** At the very least, this will cut the information on each slide by half. More likely, the exercise will help you capture the essence of what you really want to say.

## STRATEGY 3. SIGNPOST LOCATION AND DIRECTION WITH GRAPHIC ORGANIZERS

How many times have you been bewildered or lost in a PowerPoint presentation—unsure of where you are, unsure of where you have been, and even more unsure as to where you are going?

> "A good plan is like a road map: It shows the final destination and usually marks the best way to get there . . ."
>
> —H. STANLEY JUDD

### Graphic Organizers

In Part One, we stressed the importance of using clear, informative headlines to give your presentation structure, logic, and flow. You can also give your viewers a sense of time, place, and direction by incorporating a graphic organizer into your presentation.

Take a simple timeline. This can easily serve as a graphic organizer for a presenter who wants to tell a chronological story starting with past achievements, moving onto current achievements, and finishing with future plans. Here, the graphic organizer is a timeline segmented into three parts: past, present, and future. Individual events or milestones can be tagged onto the central timeline as you progress through the presentation.

### Use PowerPoint's Build and Color Features

PowerPoint's build and color features makes it simple to highlight what step or part of the visual you want your views to zoom in on.

# Graphic Organizers

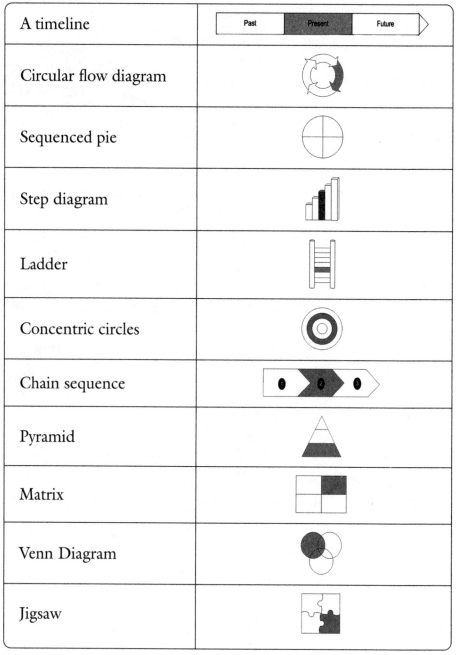

| | |
|---|---|
| A timeline | Past / Present / Future |
| Circular flow diagram | |
| Sequenced pie | |
| Step diagram | |
| Ladder | |
| Concentric circles | |
| Chain sequence | |
| Pyramid | |
| Matrix | |
| Venn Diagram | |
| Jigsaw | |

## STRATEGY 4. WHEREVER POSSIBLE, PERSUADE WITH VISUALS

### PowerPoint Is Primarily a Visual Tool

Never forget, PowerPoint is first and foremost a visual tool. PowerPoint's persuasive power comes primarily from its ability to display high-impact visuals. Yet all too often, we see PowerPoints filled with endless bullet points.

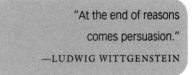

"At the end of reasons comes persuasion."
—LUDWIG WITTGENSTEIN

### Visuals Move Audiences

Great visuals are riveting. They can be the difference between success and failure in an important PowerPoint presentation. Seventy-five percent of what we learn comes to us through our eyes, 13 percent through our ears, and 12 percent through smell, taste, and touch. The University of Minnesota and 3M research discovered that the presenters who use visuals are 43 percent more persuasive than those who don't.

### Visuals Increase Message Retention

Visuals increase memorability. Most listeners forget what a speaker says within minutes of leaving a presentation. But they do remember a visual—in graphic detail—weeks, even months later.

### HOT TIPS

- **Condense all your text to its bare essentials.** Lean text is much easier to digest and remember.

- **Convert words into visuals wherever possible.** Visualize your:

  - **Facts.** Start by gridding your facts into a table.

- **Procedures.** Ask how you could draw this procedure as a series of steps.

- **Processes.** First lay the process out as a simple flow chart.

- **Principles.** Try simulating the principle as a visual model.

- **Concepts.** Initially, search for a simple visual analogy.

## STRATEGY 5. PURGE ALL BUT ESSENTIAL TEXT AND AUDIOVISUAL EFFECTS

### Less Is More

> "Genius is the ability to reduce the complicated to the simple."
>
> —C. W. CERAM

In PowerPoint, less is more. If you fill your slide with screeds of text, you make it impossible for your viewer's brain's visual channel to absorb and interpret your visuals.

On-screen text should be kept to an absolute minimum. Wherever possible, move text off screen and incorporate the words into your narration.

### Interesting but Extraneous Information Distracts

Too much screen text overload is only part of the problem. In an attempt to entertain and add interest, some presenters love adding in extra sounds, music, pictures, and animations.

While many of these "extras" add interest, too often they distract the audience and divert their attention away from the central message toward irrelevant material. The result: reduced persuasion.

### Ban Clip Art

The worst example of extraneous add-ins that distract are pieces of animated clip art. Brightly colored cartoon characters, bobbing around in the bottom right-hand corner rarely, if ever, add value.

I love Nicholas Oulton's acronym for CLIPART—**C**rass **L**ittle **In**serted **P**ictures **A**lways **R**ubbish & **T**rite.

## HOT TIPS

- **Cut all on-screen text that you intend to narrate.** Use key phrases or slogans on screen to capture the essence of your words.

- **Remove all audiovisual elements that do not support your central message.** Slash all extraneous video clips, music, sounds, animated gifs, and clipart.

- **Critically look at your templates.** Abstract, heavy, pictorial backgrounds or animated slides can confuse or distract your audience from your key points. Wherever possible, limit the animation on your slide template to your title.

- **Remove all corporate logos except the one on the title page.** They simply create additional clutter and visual overload.

- **Present like a television news station.** When CBS or other television stations present the news, they use animated effects and sound to grab attention and create impact. However, once the newsreader or broadcaster starts talking, animations are reduced to a bare minimum. All attention focuses on the broadcaster and content.

## STRATEGY 6. DICE AND SEQUENCE COMPLEX VISUALS

### Complex Diagrams Cause Confusion

"Simplicity is the ultimate sophistication."

—LEONARDO DA VINCI

Complex diagrams presented as Power-Point confuse and irritate most audiences. After all, complex diagrams can contain five or more component parts, each of which has to be understood before the main idea of the diagram can be fully grasped.

### One Point Per Slide

The rule of thumb for presenters of complex visuals is, if the diagram consists of five component parts, present the diagram as five separate slides.

Remember, it takes the same amount of time to present five points on a slide as it does to present one point on five slides.

### Stay in Control

Once you break a complex graphic into a series of slide bites, you can control what the audience watch and the order of the points you wish to make. This puts you, the presenter, firmly in control.

Sequencing the slides allows you to manage the sequence and flow of information.

## One Point Per Slide

In the slide sequence shown below, a single graphic (Slide Three) has been broken into three slides. This allows the presenter to sequence and control the flow of information and thereby increase the persuasive impact of the critical point that a large deficit looms ahead.

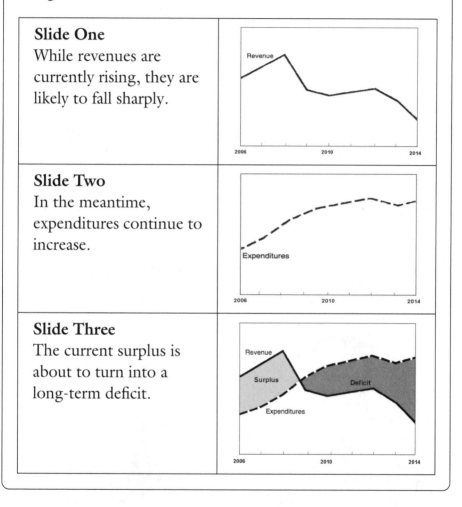

**Slide One**
While revenues are currently rising, they are likely to fall sharply.

**Slide Two**
In the meantime, expenditures continue to increase.

**Slide Three**
The current surplus is about to turn into a long-term deficit.

"What software would you recommend to give
my presentation so much flash and sizzle that
nobody notices that I have nothing to say?"

# CHAPTER NINE

# SAY IT WITH COLOR: TAPPING INTO THE POWER OF THE RAINBOW

. . . . . . . . . . . .

*"I cannot pretend to feel impartial about colors. I rejoice with the brilliant ones and am genuinely sorry for the poor browns."*

—SIR WINSTON CHURCHILL

As Walt Disney often reminded us, we live in a "wonderful world of color." PowerPoint offers a vast range of coordinated color options within its template selection.

Because of the literally millions of color choices, presenters need to understand why some colors work and why other color combinations don't. To persuade effectively, you also need to understand the psychology of color and how to adapt your color choice to a particular audience.

## INFLUENCING WITH COLOR

A 3M study found color was one of the prime reasons presentation visuals have such a big impact compared to black and

*"Colors speak all languages."*

—JOSEPH ADDISON

white. Color can add impact, create interest, and focus the eye.

### Color Persuades

We use color to inform and persuade. Red traffic lights tell us to stop. Pink suggests romance. Hunter green, seen so often in banks and legal offices, indicates permanence and value.

Color advertisements attract up to 80 percent more readers. Sales of advertised products increase by over 50 percent when color is used. The retention of the ad content increases 55 to 80 percent with color.

### Colors Evoke Emotions

Nothing evokes a mood quicker than color. Colors stimulate an emotional response. Color combinations can smooth, stimulate or charm. Reds and yellows tend to be evocative; green suggests health and prosperity. One of the most popular slide background colors, especially for business presentations, is navy blue. Navy blue suggests dependability, authority, and reliability.

### Too Many Colors Confuse

The biggest mistake presenters make with color is to use many colors. Too many colors cause confusion. Two different colors of text with one background color usually works best. To unify your presentation, it usually pays to use the same background color for all of your visuals.

# Color Associations

The color we select affects us subconsciously and communicates subliminal signals about mood. Here are some of the common meanings we associate with different colors.

| COLOR | ASSOCIATION |
| --- | --- |
| Black | authority, death, strength, loyalty, mystery |
| Blue | dependability, faith, cold, award, truth, tenderness |
| Brown | action, earthiness, autumn, fellowship |
| Green | envy, health, friendship, leisure, youthfulness |
| Red | power, passion, heat, excitement, love, fulfilment |
| Orange | warmth, action, power, valor, aggression, fury |
| Purple | dignity, royalty, frugality, melancholy |
| White | holiness, cleanliness, purity, professionalism |
| Yellow | confidence, knowledge, esteem, playfulness, friendly |

# PICKING THE RIGHT COLOR

## Tailor Your Colors to Your Audience

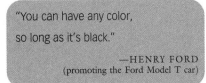

"You can have any color, so long as it's black."

—HENRY FORD
(promoting the Ford Model T car)

Different colors mean different things to different audiences. A skilled presenter will tailor the presentation colors to cater to the biases of the audience.

## Red and Green

To an accountant, green represents money and positive connotations. Red ink represents losses and has bad negative associations. For a surgeon, red (blood) is positive, green (necrosis) is negative.

## Business Blue

In business presentations, most persuaders play it safe using conservative corporate blue. It usually pays to sick with "safe" colors. Create flow with a fresh design and high impact visuals.

## Cultural Challenges

Different cultures prefer and relate to different colors. So be careful when you present in overseas countries.

# How Different Audiences Interpret Colors

|  | Movie Audience | Financial Managers | Health Care Professionals | Control Engineers |
|---|---|---|---|---|
| **Blue** | Tender | Corporate, Reliable | Dead | Cold, water |
| **Cyan** | Leisurely | Cool, subdued | Cyanotic, deprived of oxygen | Steam |
| **Green** | Playful | Profitable | Infected, bilious | Nominal, safe |
| **Yellow** | Happy | Highlighted item, important | Jaundiced | Caution |
| **Red** | Exciting | Unprofitable | Healthy | Danger |
| **Magenta** | Sad | Wealthy | Cause for concern | Hot, radioactive |

Source: Gerald E. Jones, *How to Lie With Charts,* Sybex 1995, p. 205.

# MANAGING COLOR IN POWERPOINT

> "You can't be at the pole and the equator at the same time. You must choose your own line, as I hope to do, and it will probably be color."
>
> —VINCENT VAN GOGH

You don't have to be a color expert to take advantage of PowerPoint's virtually unlimited color choices.

## Background and Foreground Elements

When thinking color in PowerPoint, remember PowerPoint manages color through two basic elements:

- The shade background colors where your chosen color appears as the background on the shades. When it comes to choosing colors, your background colors will be your most important choice.

- The foreground colors (all the other colors shown as text, lines, diagrams charts and bullets). The foreground color elements appear on top of the background. These elements include the text, lines, bullets, diagrams, and Auto Shapes.

## Contrast Is Critical

For sharp, readable PowerPoint slides, your background and foreground colors should contrast. This means you should use:

- Light text on a dark background

- Dark text on a light background

Conversely, you should avoid using:

- Similar text and background colors

- Dark text on a dark background color

## MODEL SLIDES

Here are thirty-two examples of PowerPoint slides that have been designed to communicate with precision and punch.

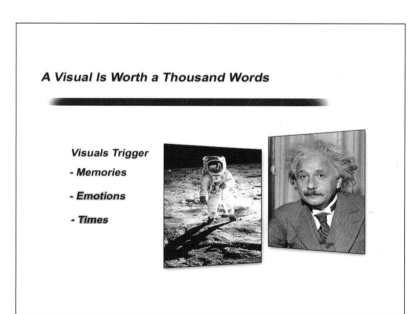

**Visuals Increase Retention**

We remember less than 10% of what we hear verbally

| | 50% |
| | 40% |
| | 30% |
| | 20% |
| | 10% |
| | 0% |

Message Retention
in Presentations

Verbal Only
Presentation

Verbal Presentation
With Visuals

Source: Wharton University Study

This slide has brilliant 3D graphics. However, the scale is difficult to read and interpret.

**A Visual Is Worth a Thousand Words**

Visuals Trigger

- Memories

- Emotions

- Times

Photos can be especially powerful when they trigger memories and emotions.

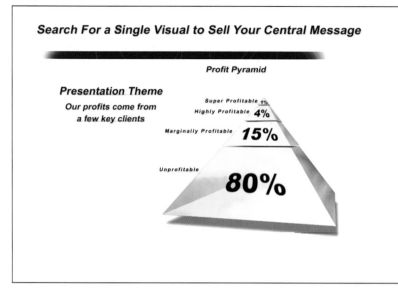

This slide uses a pyramid as a graphic organizer.

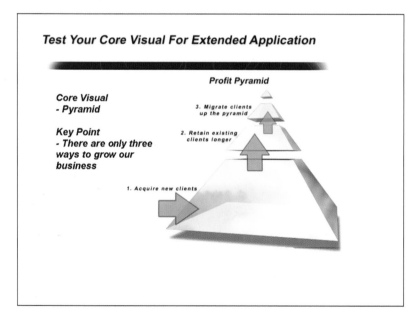

A whole presentation can be organized around a single graphic organizer such as a pyramid.

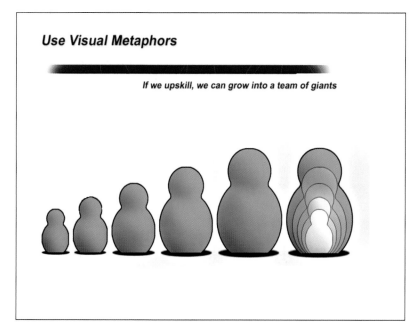

The Russian Doll metaphor is the perfect image for a presentation on building a team of giants.

The paint pots and clever use of text makes this an enticing opening slide.

## Choose Your Background Color First

On a light background dark colors stand out

On a dark background light colors stand out

The most important color decision you make in PowerPoint is your choice of background color.

## Determine The Feel You Want

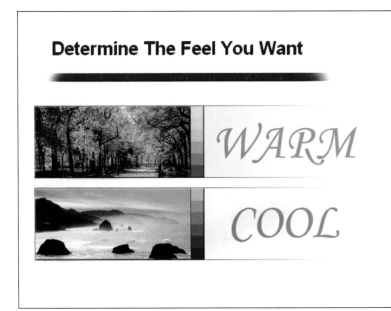

WARM

COOL

Because colors can be warm or cool, they can have a major impact on the feel and mood of your presentation.

# Use Color To Create Mood

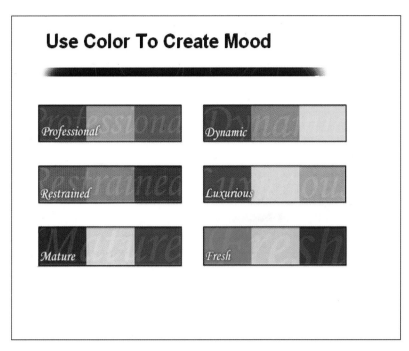

These color choices dramatically illustrate the impact color has on mood.

# Stunning Graphics

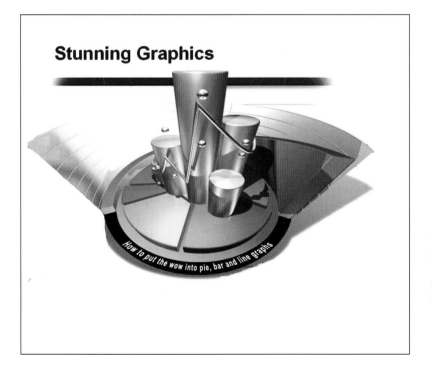

Slideshows need a powerful opening slide. This slide uses a 3D graphic to create anticipation.

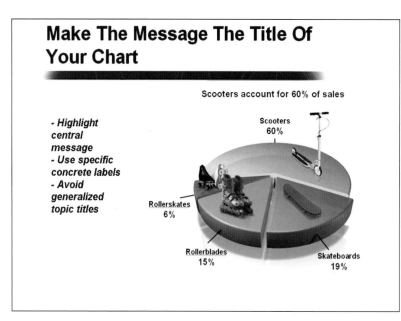

## Make The Message The Title Of Your Chart

Scooters account for 60% of sales

- Highlight central message
- Use specific concrete labels
- Avoid generalized topic titles

Scooters 60%

Rollerskates 6%

Rollerblades 15%

Skateboards 19%

The clever addition of 3D pictures of scooters, rollerblades, rollerskates, and skateboards on the top of the actual pie makes this a stunning graph.

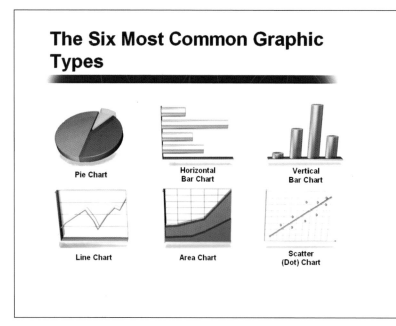

## The Six Most Common Graphic Types

Pie Chart

Horizontal Bar Chart

Vertical Bar Chart

Line Chart

Area Chart

Scatter (Dot) Chart

Six graphs on a single slide could be visual mishmash. But the simplicity amd clarity of the graphs makes this slide easy to absorb.

# Use Pie Charts For Percentages

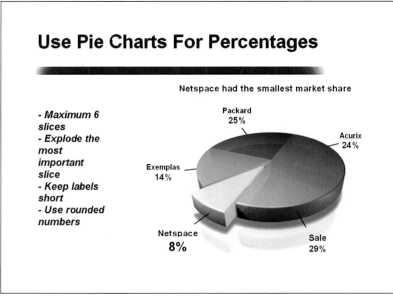

Netspace had the smallest market share

- Maximum 6 slices
- Explode the most important slice
- Keep labels short
- Use rounded numbers

Packard 25%
Acurix 24%
Exemplas 14%
Netspace 8%
Sale 29%

Powerful graphics focus your attention. Here the designer focuses your attention by exploding the key slice.

# Use Horizontal Bar Charts To Compare Magnitudes

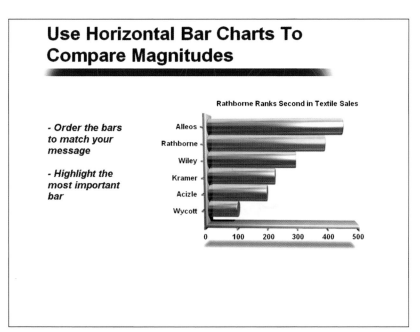

Rathborne Ranks Second in Textile Sales

- Order the bars to match your message

- Highlight the most important bar

Alleos
Rathborne
Wiley
Kramer
Acizle
Wycott

0   100   200   300   400   500

This graph is easy to understand and interpret by the way the bars are ordered and the use of color.

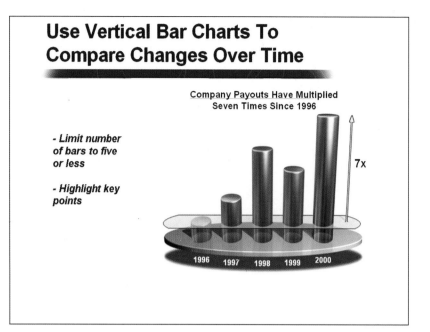

# Use Vertical Bar Charts To Compare Changes Over Time

**Company Payouts Have Multiplied Seven Times Since 1996**

- *Limit number of bars to five or less*

- *Highlight key points*

7x

1996  1997  1998  1999  2000

This chart is made easy to interpret by the way it focuses on the key point.

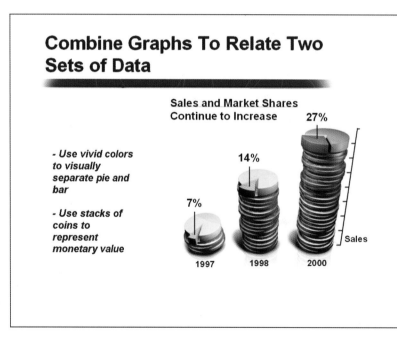

# Combine Graphs To Relate Two Sets of Data

**Sales and Market Shares Continue to Increase**

27%

- *Use vivid colors to visually separate pie and bar*

14%

- *Use stacks of coins to represent monetary value*

7%

Sales

1997  1998  2000

This slide shows how good design can communicate a complex idea with clarity.

## Use Pictorial Enhancements To Add Interest

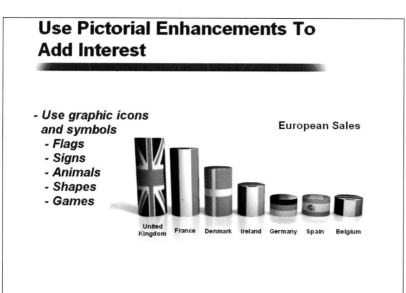

- *Use graphic icons and symbols*
  - *Flags*
  - *Signs*
  - *Animals*
  - *Shapes*
  - *Games*

**European Sales**

United Kingdom   France   Denmark   Ireland   Germany   Spain   Belgium

The 3D pictorial enhancements make this a compelling image.

## Use Vector Drawing Software To Add Realism

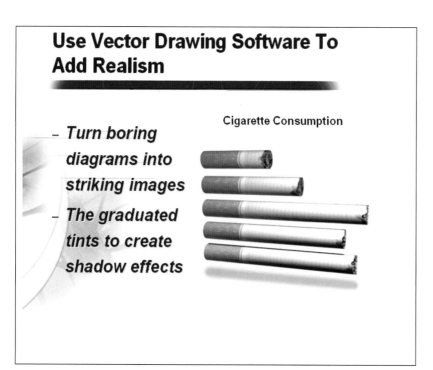

- *Turn boring diagrams into striking images*
- *The graduated tints to create shadow effects*

**Cigarette Consumption**

Imagine this image presented as a standard horizontal bar chart.

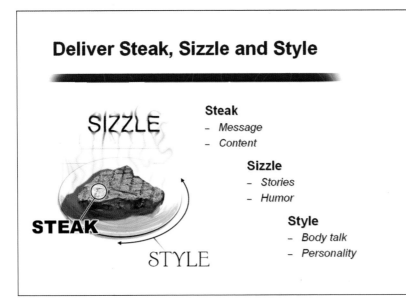

## Deliver Steak, Sizzle and Style

SIZZLE

STEAK

STYLE

**Steak**
- *Message*
- *Content*

**Sizzle**
- *Stories*
- *Humor*

**Style**
- *Body talk*
- *Personality*

The text without the plate of steak would be bland and uninviting.

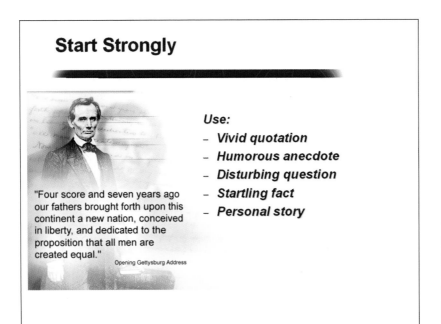

## Start Strongly

"Four score and seven years ago our fathers brought forth upon this continent a new nation, conceived in liberty, and dedicated to the proposition that all men are created equal."
Opening Gettysburg Address

*Use:*
- **Vivid quotation**
- **Humorous anecdote**
- **Disturbing question**
- **Startling fact**
- **Personal story**

The image of Abe Lincoln plus a quote from the Gettysburg address gives this slide added interest and credibility.

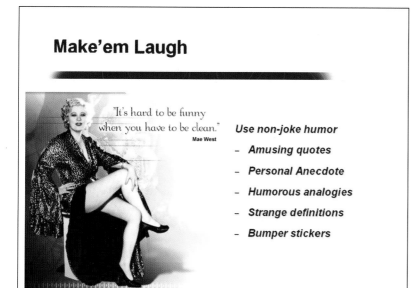

**Make'em Laugh**

"It's hard to be funny when you have to be clean."
*Mae West*

*Use non-joke humor*
- *Amusing quotes*
- *Personal Anecdote*
- *Humorous analogies*
- *Strange definitions*
- *Bumper stickers*

The "sexy" photo of Mae West combined with one of her most popular quotes reinforces the central message of this slide.

**Finish In Style**

"That's All There Is, There Isn't Any More"
Ethel Barrymore, Curtain Call, 1904

- *Signal your ending*
- *Keep it brief*
- *Finish with a memorable last line*

An appropriate photo plus a relevant quote transforms what could be a bland list of bullet points into a memorable slide.

## Use 3D Drawings to Visualize Reality

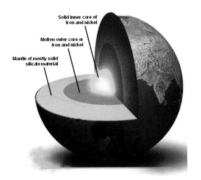

- Draw globe with 3D program

- Add further details with photo manipulating software

- Use easily readable PowerPoint text

Solid inner core of iron and nickel

Molten outer core of iron and nickel

Mantle of mostly solid silicate material

A skilled designer can dramatically increase the impact of a visual with 3D.

## Analyze Your Audience

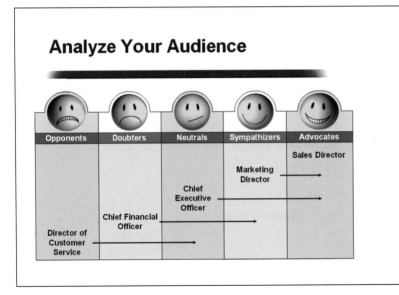

| Opponents | Doubters | Neutrals | Sympathizers | Advocates |
|---|---|---|---|---|
| | | | | Sales Director |
| | | | Marketing Director | |
| | | Chief Executive Officer | | |
| | Chief Financial Officer | | | |
| Director of Customer Service | | | | |

This table would be bland and would lack impact if it weren't for the smiling and grimacing cartoon faces.

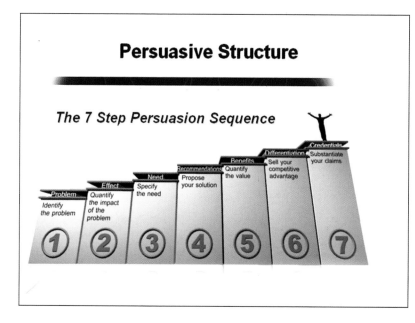

PowerPoint viewers like to know where they're heading. This step diagram clearly communicates the seven steps to persuasion success.

The use of stopwatch imagery adds pizzazz.

## Tune Into Station WII-FM

- Sell benefits, not features

- Visualize each benefit

- Customize each benefit

This slide shows how a skilled designer can add extra visual punch to a well-known simple sales acronym – **WIIFM**.

## Use Persuasive Words

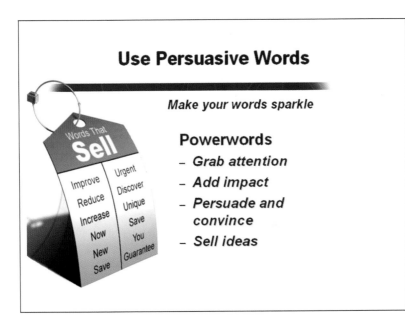

*Make your words sparkle*

**Powerwords**
– *Grab attention*
– *Add impact*
– *Persuade and convince*
– *Sell ideas*

Words That
**Sell**

| | |
|---|---|
| Improve | Urgent |
| Reduce | Discover |
| Increase | Unique |
| Now | Save |
| New | You |
| Save | Guarantee |

Imagine this slide without the use of the price tag.

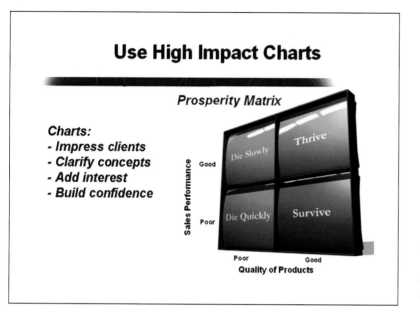

This matrix chart looks impressive and makes what could be a difficult concept appear simple.

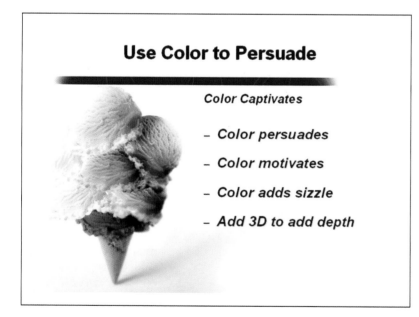

The colors in this slide really do captivate. The 3D gives the image depth plus added realism.

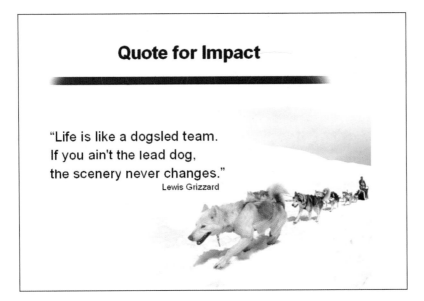

**Quote for Impact**

"Life is like a dogsled team.
If you ain't the lead dog,
the scenery never changes."
Lewis Grizzard

The humorous quote and supporting imagery make this a powerful slide.

**Success**

The photo works on two levels:
(1) It reinforces the central message.
(2) It delivers emotional punch.

## HOT TIPS

Here are some broad guidelines when selecting colors.

**Step One: Assess your audience.** Ask what makes this audience distinctive?

**Step Two: Select the mood** you want to create with your color scheme.

**Step Three: Select a dominant or primary color** which reflects that mood. Consider making this your background slide color.

**Step Four: Select one or two support colors.**

**Step Five: Test your color combination** for overall impact in a mini slideshow.

"You have been accused of cruel and abusive behavior.
Is it true you made your staff sit through
a PowerPoint presentation?"

# CHAPTER TEN

# BULLETS, BULLETS, AND MORE BULLETS: HOW TO WRITE, USE, AND LAY OUT COMPELLING TEXT

• • • • • • • • • • • •

"You can stroke people with words."

—F. SCOTT FITZGERALD

PowerPoint slideshows that consist of endless bulleted text are persuasion killers. Nevertheless, text can be used artfully and persuasively.

However, it doesn't matter how elegant or impressive your type is if your text is not readable.

## TERRIFIC TEXT

The most common PowerPoint presentation is largely text. The way you format and present your text will have a big impact on your presentation.

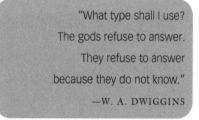

"What type shall I use?
The gods refuse to answer.
They refuse to answer
because they do not know."

—W. A. DWIGGINS

### What is a Typeface?

A typeface is a family of letters of all the same design. A typeface consists of a mix of fonts which include bold and italic. Times New Roman is a typeface. Times New Roman Bold Italic is a font.

## Type Styles

Typefaces can be broken into two basic groups: *serif* and *sans serif.* Serif faces have small finishing strokes or "tails" at the ends of their letters. Typefaces without finishing strokes or "tails" are called sans serif faces.

## Serif Type

Designers choose serif typefaces because they are easy to read. Our eyes find it easy to follow the baselines of serif type. By far the most popular serif type is Times New Roman.

## Sans Serif Type

Some PowerPoint designers prefer sans serif faces because of their clean uncluttered look. The most popular PowerPoint sans serif font is Arial.

## HOT TIPS

- **Consider using Tahoma or Verdana as an alternative to Arial as your prime typeface.** They work just as well as Arial and look fresher.

- **As an alternative to Times New Roman, try Georgia.** It looks clean, is crisp, and is easy to read.

- **Avoid using multiple typefaces.** One typeface is usually enough to support a presentation.

- **Use two typefaces where you want to add variety and contrast.** Use the first for the headlines and use the second for the body copy. Consider using Tahoma for the headline and Georgia for the text.

- **If you can't avoid using lots of text, use a serif face for all your body text.** It is easier to read an extended amount of text in a serif typeface.

## TYPE, SIZE, AND STYLE

One of the biggest design sins of Power-Point creators is to make text too large or too small. Type that is too large looks ugly and clumsy. Type that is too small looks cramped and can't be read.

> "Does fashion matter?
> Only if you're out of it."
>
> —KIM CAMPBELL

### Changing Font Size

Changing font size in PowerPoint is easy so you can decrease or increase the font size buttons until the slide looks right. One inch contains 72 points. As a rule of thumb:

- Make titles 24 to 36 points.

- Make text 18 to 24 points.

### Line Spacing

Line spacing has a big impact on readability. Single line spacing looks cramped on a PowerPoint, so you need to increase the line spacing to 1.2 or 1.5 points. PowerPoint design templates will automatically space your text out in a visually appealing way.

### Readability and Legibility

Readability refers to whether a block of text is easy to read. Legibility refers to whether a short burst of text—such as a headline or danger sign—is instantly recognizable. Research shows while serif typefaces are more readable, sans serif typefaces such as Tahoma, are more recognizable.

## HOT TIPS

- **Bold text is the most useful special effect. It's a great way to highlight key words or points.** But remember, highlighting works best when it is used discreetly. Also, extra-bold type is less readable than a regular typeface.

- **Underlining text can be very useful if you want to show changes in a paragraph.** But again, be discreet.

- **Italicized text often looks great on the computer screen but is often unreadable when projected.** Because italicized text is more difficult to read than normal text, the type size may need to be enlarged.

- **Consider using drop shadows to give your text the extra depth it sometimes needs to standout on a slide.** But again, be discreet with its use.

- **Increase your line spacing if your line length is longer than eight words.** The extra line spacing makes it easier for the viewer to separate individual words.

## BULLET LAYOUT AND DESIGN

### The Benefit of Bullets

Bulleted text helps us:

> "If it is possible to cut a word out, cut it out."
>
> —GEORGE ORWELL

- Break up blocks of information into scannable links.

- Focus our attention.

- Organize our content into a logical order.

- Add structure to layouts.

Yet few presentation designers give much thought at all to how they use bullets. They should, because bullet choice and bullet placement can have significant impact on the final look and feel of a slide.

## Bullet List Fundamentals

The fundamentals for bullet use are:

- Limit your list length to six or fewer points. Lists with more than six items look cramped and crowded.

- One list per slide. Multiple lists confuse audiences. Center the list on the slide with lots of white space above and below the list.

- If your bulleted points are no more than one line in length, keep spacing at the "1 line" spacing option in PowerPoint. For larger entities, increase line spacing.

## HOT TIPS

- **Unless there is a compelling reason, stick with the regular circle and square bullet points.** In most cases, they look more professional.

- **Make your bullets the same size as the text type.** But some designers think bullets look better when they are one or two points less the rest of the text.

- **Don't place your text hard up against the bullet.** Add at least one extra space between a bullet and the text.

- **Consider coloring the bullet to add visual interest.** Dark red and blue bullets always look good with black text.

- **Align lists on the left vertically.** Leave the right margin ragged or unjustified.

## WRITING COMPELLING BULLETS

The most boring and least effective PowerPoint slides consist of bulleted lists of long, grammatically correct sentences. PowerPoint word lists should rarely if ever be written as full sentences. Word lists should be written as short, punchy statements.

Compare these two examples:

**Original sentence:**

The gains include increased sales, reductions in cost and an increase in customer loyalty.

**Edited bulleted sentence:**

*Gains*

- Higher sales

- Reduced costs

- Increased customer loyalty

The ideal bullet statement should be no more than six words and fit into a single line.

## HOT TIPS

- **Place the most important points at the top of the list.** That's where viewers look for them.

- **Slash all unnecessary words.** Change "reduction in working capital" to "reduced working capital."

- **Capitalize the first letter in a list.** But never use all caps for an entire entry or list.

- **Don't punctuate lists with periods or full stops.** Most slides don't need them to separate out blocks of text.

- **Replace bullets with numbers where the order is critical for meaning.** Step, by step instructions usually need numbers to make sense.

- **Consider adding a background image to add visual variety to the text.** Photo object illustrations work best.

## USING TEXT BUILDS

### Boring Text Slides

Have you ever watched the glazed look of boredom that descends across an audience when a presenter starts delivering a succession of bullet-text slides?

To make matters worse, in most bullet slide presentations, the audience races ahead of the presenter. While the presenter is still talking about the first bullet, the audience skims down the slide to read the rest of the slide.

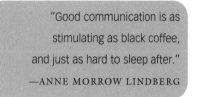

"Good communication is as stimulating as black coffee, and just as hard to sleep after."
—ANNE MORROW LINDBERG

### Use the Animations Feature

To overcome bullet tedium and uncontrolled read-ahead, you can use PowerPoint's animation feature. By using the animations feature you can command your bullets to appear magically one at a time.

### Using Builds

For example, if you have three bullets on a slide, you can hide the last two bullets while you talk about the first bullet. When you finish talking about the first bullet point, you then command the second bullet to magically appear. An example is laid out on the page opposite.

As a result, your audience stays focused on the current item you are addressing. Plus, moving text images create visual interest.

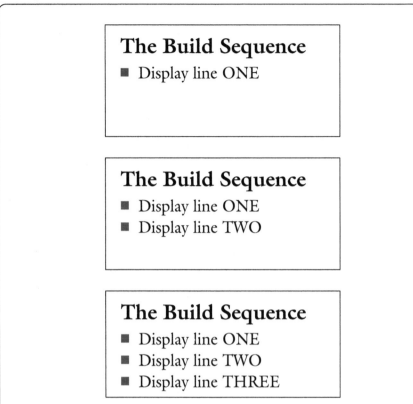

## TEXT OR IMAGES

So, which one is the more potent when it comes to persuasion—text or visuals? The answer is: It depends.

### The Two Paths to Persuasion

Persuasion is the process of changing or reinforcing attitudes, beliefs, or behavior. We respond to persuasive messages in two ways: thoughtfully and mindlessly.

### Thoughtful Persuasion

When we are thoughtful, we listen hard to what the persuader is saying; we weigh the pros and cons of each argument.

We critique the message for logic and consistency. And if we don't like what we hear, we ask questions and call for more information. When we are in thoughtful mode, the persuasiveness of the message is determined by the merits of the case.

## Mindless Persuasion

When we respond to messages mindlessly, our brains are locked on automatic. We don't have the time, motivation, or ability to listen intently.

So instead of relying on facts, logic, and evidence to make a judgment, we take a mental shortcut, and rely on our instincts to provide us with cues on how to respond.

If your presentation is information-heavy, requires thoughtful consideration, and involves logic and evidence, you will need to use text-based slides.

If your presentation is primarily about changing moods and perceptions, increase the ratio of images to text.

"At the request of those who are following a low-carb diet,
my pie chart has been replaced by a steak chart."

# CHAPTER ELEVEN

# COMPELLING CHARTS: HOW TO PUT THE WOW INTO PIE, BAR, AND LINE GRAPHS

• • • • • • • • • • • •

"Statistics will prove anything, even the truth."

—NOËL MOYNIHAN

The right chart used at the right time with the right audience can convince the most skeptical of audiences.

PowerPoint comes loaded with features that allow you to optimize a chart's impact.

## PERSUADING WITH CHARTS

### Select the Appropriate Chart

There are seven common chart types. These are:

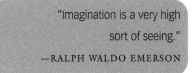

"Imagination is a very high sort of seeing."

—RALPH WALDO EMERSON

1. Pie charts

2. Horizontal bar charts

3. Vertical or column charts

4. Line charts

5. Area charts

6. Dot charts (or scatter diagrams)

7. Tables

## Pinpoint the Relationship

To choose the best graph form, first pinpoint the relationship you want to emphasize.

For example, if you want to plot a trend, you should first consider a line gap. If you want to compare changes in quantities over time you should first consider an area chart.

## Choose Your Title

Headings should help your viewer to interpret the chart. So wherever possible, interpret the graph for your audience and make the message the title of your chart.

The broad general heading on the chart opposite means this chart can be interpreted in at least four different ways. The best title is the key point you want your audience to remember.

## Make the Message the Title

The broad general heading on the chart below means this chart can be interpreted in at least four different ways.

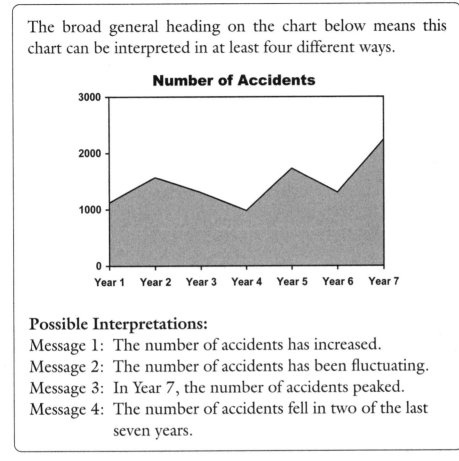

**Possible Interpretations:**

Message 1:  The number of accidents has increased.

Message 2:  The number of accidents has been fluctuating.

Message 3:  In Year 7, the number of accidents peaked.

Message 4:  The number of accidents fell in two of the last seven years.

# USE PIE CHARTS FOR PERCENTAGES

Pies are for percentages. However, you can also use a pie chart to illustrate any proportional relationship between a segment and a whole pie.

## Highlight the Key Slice

Some presenters make the mistake of "cutting their pie" into too many pieces. When a pie comprises more than six pieces, it becomes very difficult to read, let alone interpret. If you have more than six slices, choose the five most important and put the rest in an "other" slice. This reduces the slices to a visually manageable number.

Position the most important slice in the top right hand position starting at one o'clock. That's where viewers first look. The importance of a slice can be emphasized further by using a contrasting shade or by exploding the slice out from the rest of the pie.

## Add 3D

Consider adding a third dimension (3D) to give the pie the impression of being solid. But beware: 3D adding will make the sections with 3D appear larger than other sections of the pie. Unethical persuaders regularly use 3D to manipulate the message they want to communicate with a pie graph.

## Emphasize the Most Important Slice

In this segmented pie chart shown below, the most important slice is positioned at the top right hand position. To reinforce the importance of the top right-hand slice, it has also been pulled out from the rest of the pie.

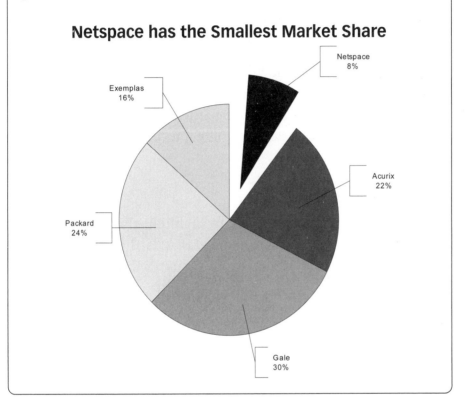

**Netspace has the Smallest Market Share**

## USE BAR CHARTS TO COMPARE MAGNITUDES

Horizontal bar charts are useful when you want to compare the size or magnitude of a group of items.

### Control the Order of the Bars

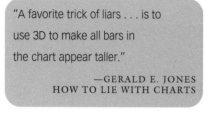

"A favorite trick of liars . . . is to use 3D to make all bars in the chart appear taller."

—GERALD E. JONES
HOW TO LIE WITH CHARTS

Most presenters preset their bars randomly. You should however, try to arrange the bars in the order that best suits the message you want to send. Randomly ordered bars can create confusion and make the graph harder to interpret. Remember, PowerPoint viewers usually have only a few seconds to interpret a graph.

### Use Contrasting Colors

Use a contrasting color or shade to highlight the most important bar and reinforce the message title. Look at the example on the opposite page. Your eye immediately focuses on the heavily shaded Rathbone bar.

### Limit the Number of Bars

If practical, keep the number of bars to five or fewer. Five or fewer bars are much easier to read and interpret. Bars can be any width. However, white space between the bars makes them easier to distinguish.

# Reinforce Your Central Message

In the bar graph shown below, the bars have been ranked from best (highest) to worst (lowest) sales. The key Rathbone bar is shaded differently to reinforce the central message.

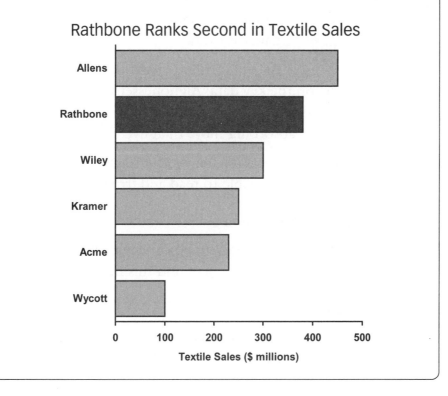

## Rathbone Ranks Second in Textile Sales

# USE COLUMN CHARTS TO COMPARE DATA CHANGES OVER TIME

## Keep It Simple

> "We are drowning in information but starved for knowledge."
>
> —JOHN NAISBITT

Column or vertical bar charts are ideal when you want to compare changes in data over time.

As with other chart forms, you should focus your viewers on the key data. All nonessential data should be pruned out. If practical, keep the number of bars to five or fewer. Viewers have trouble absorbing more than five bars.

Make sure the labels read horizontally rather than vertically. Vertical labels are virtually impossible to read and irritate audiences.

## Make It Easier for the Viewer

Use shadings, color arrows, or a graphical device when you want to stress a particular point. Audiences find this helpful.

## Subdivided Column Graphs

Use subdivided column charts when you want to show how the components make up the total change over time. But don't use more than five components in a subdivided column chart. More than five makes the chart difficult to interpret.

## Highlight the Key Message

In this column graph, the arrow helps highlight the central message and focus the viewer on your key point.

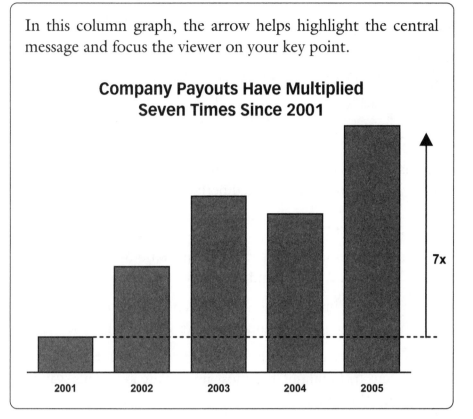

**Company Payouts Have Multiplied Seven Times Since 2001**

# USE LINE CHARTS TO PLOT TRENDS

## Plotting Trends

"What is now proved was once only imagin'd."

—WILLIAM BLAKE

Line charts are the most popular of all chart forms, and are ideal when you want to plot or highlight a trend in the data. Of all chart forms, line charts are the easiest to read and interpret.

Line charts are also useful when you have lots of figures you want to plot over multiple or extended periods of time.

## Highlight the Trend Line

With line charts, make sure the trend line is bolder than the baseline of the graph. A bold trend line helps focus viewer attention.

Where possible, limit the number of trend lines to two or three. More than three and the graph looks like visual spaghetti.

In a multiple line chart, use the most contrasting color or the boldest solid line to highlight the most important line. This way you stay in control of the message.

## Highlight the Key Trend Line

This index scale line chart quickly shows the relative change between profits and costs since 1996. The solid line is used to highlight the most important item—profits.

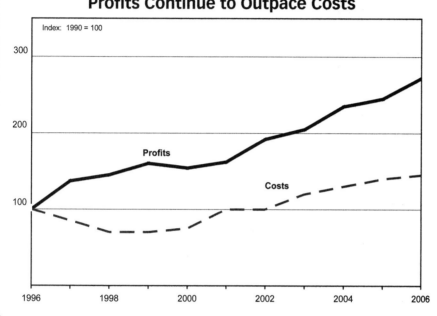

**Profits Continue to Outpace Costs**

Index: 1990 = 100

## USE AREA CHARTS TO COMPARE CHANGES IN QUANTITIES OVER TIME

Area charts are essentially filled-in line graphs. They are useful when you want to compare a change in quantities over time.

### Anchor the Graph

With area charts, make sure the bottom layer takes up the largest share of the graph. The largest share thus visually anchors the graph and makes it easier to interpret.

Use your darkest color to show your base. Also, keep your labels horizontal. Vertical labels are simply too difficult to read at the back of a room.

### Allow Extra Time for Viewing

Area charts are most difficult to interpret than pie and bar charts, so give your audience extra time for comprehension.

## Anchor Your Graph

The dark bottom layer anchors the graph and highlights the huge contribution consulting makes to profits. The thick bold line keeps the primary emphasis on the total.

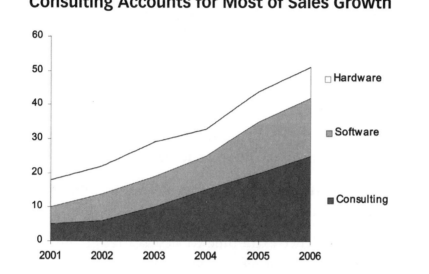

**Consulting Accounts for Most of Sales Growth**

## USE SCATTER OR DOT CHARTS TO SHOW RELATIONSHIP PATTERNS

### When to Use Scatter Charts

> "Garbage in, garbage out."
>
> —SAYING (AMERICAN)

Scatter charts or dot graphs show whether or not the relationship between two variables follows an expected pattern.

If your presentation includes phrases like *related to, changes with,* and *varies with,* you should consider adding a scatter chart.

### Do's and Don'ts

- Don't use scatter charts on nontechnical audiences. They are usually too difficult to interpret accurately.

- Keep the message as simple as possible. Scatter graphs can easily confuse even highly educated audiences.

- Give your audience extra time to view scatter graphs. A scatter graph takes twice as long as a bar or pie graph to comprehend.

## Keep the Message Simple

In this scatter chart, the dots cluster around the expected pattern, showing there is a relationship between spending on research and profit levels.

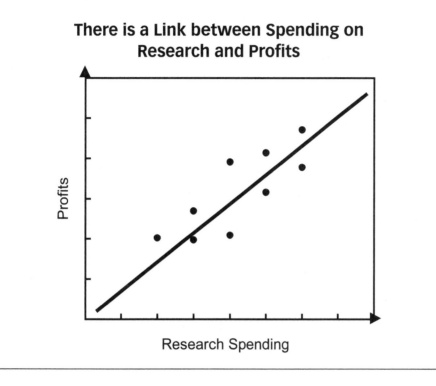

**There is a Link between Spending on Research and Profits**

Profits

Research Spending

# USE TABLES TO SUMMARIZE DATA

### Charts with Data

> "Round numbers are always false."
>
> —SAMUEL JOHNSON

Tables are charts with data arranged in rows and columns to allow side-by-side comparisons. Tables are often the best way to communicate masses of numbers and data for which graphing would be inappropriate.

### Formatting Tables

There is no one right way to format a table. The best format depends on the type of data, the amount of data, and the purpose of the table.

When formatting tables, use as few graphic elements as possible to grid the data. Often the easiest way to improve the look of a table is to remove unnecessary borders and gridlines.

### Ration Your Use of Bold

Presenters commonly create visual confusion by bolding all of the numbers. Limit your use of bold to the headers and key data.

When you grid your data, make it visually obvious to your viewer whether they should first read down the rows from top to bottom, or read across the slide from left to right.

# Use Gantt Charts for Scheduling

Tables used for scheduling are often referred to as Gantt charts. A Gantt chart is a table that is used for planning and monitoring procedures. The test for a Gantt chart is how well it communicates when procedures take place. Below is a simple Gantt chart used by a book publisher.

## Book Publication Schedule

| Week | January | | | | February | | | | March | | | | April | | | |
|---|---|---|---|---|---|---|---|---|---|---|---|---|---|---|---|---|
| | 1 | 2 | 3 | 4 | 5 | 6 | 7 | 8 | 9 | 10 | 11 | 12 | 13 | 14 | 15 | 16 |
| Writing | ■ | ■ | ■ | ■ | ■ | ■ | ■ | ■ | | | | | | | | |
| Editing | | | | | | | | | ■ | ■ | | | | | | |
| Design | | | | ■ | ■ | ■ | ■ | ■ | | | | | | | | |
| Typesetting | | | | | | | | | | | ■ | ■ | ■ | ■ | | |
| Printing | | | | | | | | | | | | | | | ■ | ■ |

"You have been accused of cruel and abusive behavior.
Is it true you made your staff sit through
a PowerPoint presentation?"

# CHAPTER TWELVE

# DIAGRAMS, PHOTOS, AND CARTOONS: HOW TO INFORM WITH IMPACT

. . . . . . . . . . . . .

*"One picture is worth a thousand words."*

—FRED R. BARNARD

Because PowerPoint is first and foremost a visual persuasion tool, presenters have to know how to select and present diagrams, photographs, and cartoons with flair.

Audiences admire and respect a presenter who goes the extra mile to make their lives easier and more enjoyable by using diagrams, photos, and cartoons.

## USING DIAGRAMS

### Simplifying and Visualizing the Complex

Diagrams are often the best way to simplify and visualize complex systems and processes.

*"Developing the plan is actually laying out the sequence of events that have to occur for you to achieve your goal.."*

—GEORGE L. MORRISEY

Think of a flow chart, a decision tree, or an organizational chart. They simplify complex ideas that are difficult to explain in words. Diagrams are especially useful for displaying sequences and cause-and-effect patterns.

### Circles, Triangles, and Rectangles

Diagrams are charts which are circles, triangles and rectangles linked by lines and arrows to show how we work and organize our lives.

Diagrams primarily use text to provide most of the explanation. Since diagrams are primarily textual and nonquantitative, numbers play a relatively small part.

### The Ideal Diagram

The ideal diagram does three things:

1. It informs.

2. It explains.

3. It simplifies.

## HOT TIPS

- **Each diagram has an underlying logic.** The logic of an organization chart is the chain of command; the logic of a flow chart is the sequence of events.

- **Keep it simple.** The musts for diagrams are simplicity and clarity.

- **Use the thirty-second test.** If you can't understand a diagram in thirty seconds, it's usually too complicated.

- **Break complicated diagrams into multiple parts.** When you plan your diagram, consider building it as a series of images. Then summarize with an overview at the end.

- **Place labels on or alongside the parts they identify rather than the legend.** Labels are complicated diagrams and are especially important.

- **Consider using a graphic artist to enhance basic images.** The addition of a little creative flair can make a simple diagram look sophisticated.

## USE ORGANIZATION CHARTS TO DISPLAY RANKINGS

### Visualizing Your Organization

Organization charts are hierarchal diagrams that show how people, operations, or activities are organized or structured.

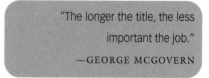

"The longer the title, the less important the job."
—GEORGE MCGOVERN

Organization charts are used to:

- Define lines of authority and responsibility.

- Show who reports to whom.

- Show how people, departments, and teams relate to each other.

The typical organization chart consists of text enclosed in boxes connected by lines or arrows. The most common type of organization charts displays how the organization hierarchy works, typically flowing from top to bottom.

## De-Emphasizing Hierarchy

If you want to de-emphasize the hierarchical nature of an organization chart, you can change the shape. Look how the circular organization chart shown below plays down the hierarchical nature of the organization by placing the president in the center rather than at the top.

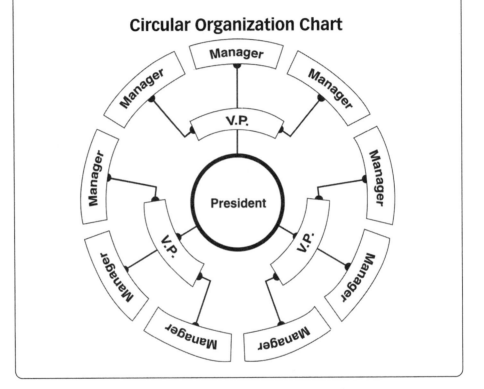

### Circular Organization Chart

# USE MATRIXES TO EXPLAIN CONCEPTS

## Displaying Concepts and Ideas

A matrix display consists of multiple charts arranged in rows and patterns. Consultants love to use matrixes to illustrate and communicate concepts and ideas.

> "There is nothing so powerful as an old idea whose time has come again."
>
> —BEN WATTENBERG

In the example shown opposite, the Boston Consulting Group (BCG) uses the Growth Matrix to show their clients the link between market growth and market share.

They clearly labeled the four matrixes: star, dog, cash cow, and question mark. The result is a powerful, compelling matrix that is still used on most introduction marketing courses across the Western world.

## Allow Extra Time to View

Matrixes take usually extra time to absorb and interpret. Give your audience thirty seconds or more to absorb the matrix.

## The Boston Matrix

The BCG Growth Matrix illustrates the impact clever labeling can make. For easy interpretation, the BCG matrix is split into four boxes. The four matrixes are labeled stars, dogs, cash cows, and question marks for easy memorability.

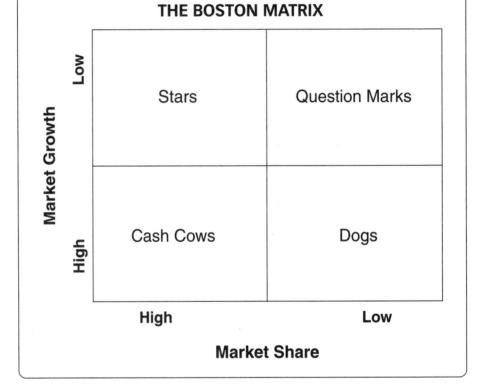

**THE BOSTON MATRIX**

## ADD ART AND ILLUSTRATIONS TO CREATE IMPACT

### Choosing the Right Image

Adding art and illustrations to your diagrams can dramatically increase their impact and persuasiveness.

> "Art is the sex of the imagination."
> —GEORGE JEAN NATHAN

The visual effect of an illustration helps your viewers remember and understand your message much more quickly. The key with illustrations and artwork is to choose the right image.

### Avoid Cheap Clip Art

Amateur presenters often clutter the presentations with irrelevant, low quality images. The worst presenters can't resist adding cheap-looking clip art to every slide.

There is a mountain of cheap or free clip art available on the Web but for important presentations, it is worthwhile paying for access to professional quality art and photographic images.

## Adding Images to a Diagram

In *The Way I See It Diagram*, photographs of a girl have been incorporated into a series of mirrors to increase the dramatic impact. Imagine how dull this diagram would be without the imagery.

**The Way I See It Diagram**

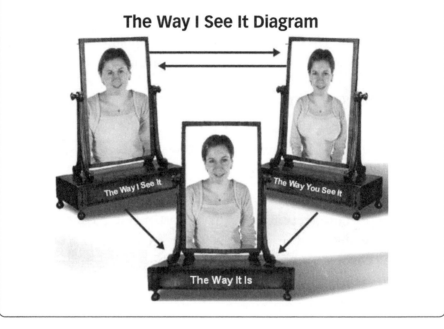

# USE STRATEGY DIAGRAMS TO PLOT TACTICS

### Simplify Complex, Abstract Ideas

Marketing professionals love to use diagrams to simplify complex and abstract
ideas.

> "Hit hard, hit fast, hit often."
> —WILLIAM F. "BULL" HALSEY

### Military Metaphor

Look at the marketing strategies diagram on the next page. It contains all the ingredients of an effective diagram. It is organized
around a military metaphor. Military metaphors are commonly
used by marketing strategists and readily understood by most audiences.

### Linking a Circle and Square

The uncluttered diagram is simply a circle and square linked by
clearly labelled arrows. The beauty of this is you can build it up as
a series of slides, adding each of these strategies as an overlay.

## Visualizing Marketing Strategies

The beauty of this marketing strategy diagram is its simplicity and clarity. Words have been kept to an absolute minimum. Yet all the information you need to use to interpret the diagram is there.

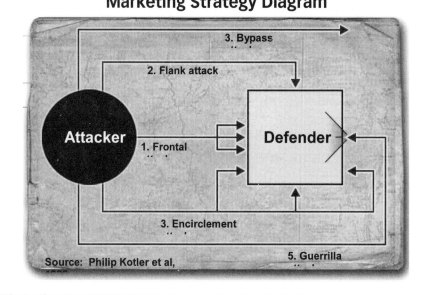

## USE VISUAL METAPHORS TO SELL IDEAS

A metaphor is an implied comparison between two points.

### Sales Funnel Metaphor

The sales funnel metaphor shown on the slide is instantly recognizable and reinforces the key point that the sales process involves chasing lots of suspects and prospects until you find the critical few that can be closed and converted to buyers. The metaphor is powerful because it instantly makes sense and aids memorability.

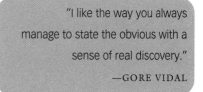

"I like the way you always manage to state the obvious with a sense of real discovery."

—GORE VIDAL

The right metaphors add visual interest and significantly increase the memorability and impact of a message. When it comes to persuasion, metaphors rate very highly in impact.

Simple, instantly recognizable shapes and symbols work best.

Use bright, clean colors. They grab attention. Also, keep your labels short and horizontal. They're easier to read.

## The Sales Funnel Metaphor

The power of the sales funnel metaphor is how it visually reinforces the key idea that for every buyer, you need to identify lots of prospects and suspects.

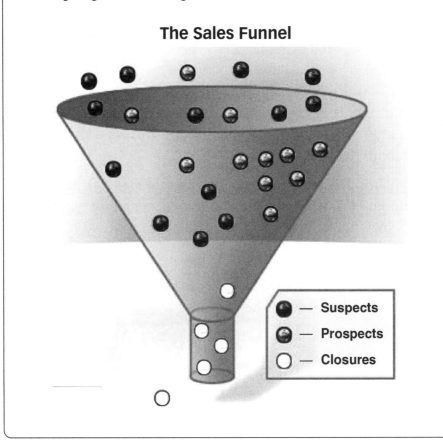

**The Sales Funnel**

## ADD IMPACT WITH PHOTOS

Cheap digital photography plus online access to millions of affordable royalty-free photographs means it is easier than ever to find the perfect photo for your Power-Point.

> "The camera cannot lie. But it can be an accessory to untruth."
>
> —HAROLD EVANS

### Reinforce Your Central Message

Presenters continue to use photos as visual wallpaper. To create impact, a photo must reinforce the central message or illustrate an important point in your slide.

Most photos need rigorous editing. Nonessential background must be cropped out. With the nonessential deleted, you can enlarge the image to add extra reinforcement to your message.

### Create Graphic Continuity

Your photos should tie in with your general storyline. If your storyline is centred on a product launch theme, then the photos should match or at least align with the theme. If your first image uses a picture of an Apollo launch, then the rest of your presentation should preferably use space imagery.

### Customize Your Imagery

Remember, photos are powerful because they evoke emotions. They can offend as easily as they can impress. Photos must, therefore, always be customized to your audience's interests and culture.

## Image Energy Gauge

When choosing photos to use in PowerPoint, use the Image Energy Gauge to guide your selection.

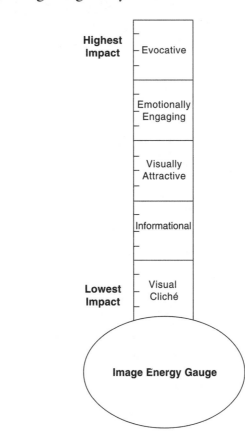

**Evocative:** Sensational. Perfect fit. One of a kind. Highest form.

**Emotionally engaging**: Tugs at the heart.

**Visually Attractive**: Graphically appealing, but does not "pull the heart strings."

**Informational**: Communicates or reinforces core message.

**Visual Cliché**: Boring. Space filler. Do not use. Lowest form.

# PRESENTING WITH CARTOONS

## Use Cartoons to Add Levity

Cartoons are a great way to add levity and put your audience at ease. Presenters who don't like using jokes or stories can usually find an appropriate cartoon from the tens of thousands available on the Internet.

> "A joke's a very serious thing."
> —CHARLES CHURCHILL

## Use Cartoons to Influence and Persuade

Cartoons, if used well, can bring much more than a touch of levity to a presentation. Because humor works on our emotions, cartoons can be an especially potent weapon when you need to deliver a controversial message to a tough audience.

## Use Cartoons to Simplify Complex Issues

Cartoons are excellent for simplifying complex issues and hammering home a telling point. Cartoons can deliver remarkably sophisticated insights into complex issues. An editorial cartoon, for example, uses caricature, parody, irony, and analogy to make its point.

Subject cartoons to the same relevance test as any other photograph or diagram. If your cartoon does not reinforce your central message, leave it out. Your cartoons must also make your audience laugh, or at the very least, make them smile.

# USE HUMOR TO PERSUADE

Cartoons work because of the way they make you smile. Professional persuaders know humor can be a powerful tool. "Humor is a powerful . . . tool," writes humor consultant Malcolm Kushner. "It can gain attention, create rapport, and make a message more memorable. It can also relieve tension, enhance relationships, and motivate people, if it is used appropriately."

## Cartoons That Add Insight

Here is an ideal cartoon for a business presentation skills trainer who wants to stress the importance of preparation. I like using cartoons by Randy Glasbergen because they communicate razor-sharp messages while always drawing a smile.

Copyright 2004 by Randy Glasbergen
www.glasbergen.com

"I gave a presentation today but I only pretended to know what I was talking about. Fortunately, my audience was only pretending to listen."

## Wit Increases Participation

"If I can get you to laugh with me," says actor John Cleese, "you like me better, which makes you more open to my ideas. And if I can persuade you to laugh at the particular point I make, by laughing at it you acknowledge its truth."

Humor increases interactivity. And interactivity increases memorability.

## How to Make Humor Relevant

The cardinal rule when using humor is to add the humor after you've planned your message and made a list of the key analyzed points you want to make. Your humor, says Kushner, should "introduce, summarize or highlight" one or more of your points."

The key point when using humor to persuade is to make it relevant. The biggest mistake unskilled persuaders made is to use irrelevant humor. To be effective, humor must make a point.

"A basic principle of audience psychology," says Kushner, "is that people resist humor if they think someone is trying to be funny. Humor reduces our resistance to the central message of the pitch. We are less likely to object or to challenge a message that is laced with humor.

Audiences are much more accepting when humor is used to make a point. Even if we don't think the speaker is funny, the "humor still makes a point and moves the presentation forward."

"A live orchestra, costumes, scenery, fireworks, jugglers, elephants, The Rockettes? Can't you just use Power Point like everyone else?"

# CHAPTER THIRTEEN

# PRESENT AND SELL: THE ULTIMATE POWERPOINT SALES PRESENTATION

. . . . . . . . . . . . .

*"Our work is the presentation of our capabilities."*

—EDWARD GIBBON

To make your PowerPoint sales presentations sing, you need to engage your audience before you attempt to persuade them with digital dazzle.

Once you have established rapport with your prospects, you need to take them step-by-step through a logical sequence that uncovers their needs and delivers a persuasive solution.

## ESTABLISH A PERSUASIVE STRUCTURE

### Selling is Persuasion

Selling is about transforming a customer problem into a need for your solution.

> *"Once you know how to control the sales process, you can begin to shape the result."*
>
> —HARRY MILLS

Selling involves persuasion. You have to sell the value of the solution. Plus, you have to persuade the customer your solution is better than your competitors' and you have the credentials to do the job.

## The Seven Steps to Persuasion

Consider using a seven step persuasion sequence for all your major PowerPoint sales presentations.

*Step 1: Identify your prospect's problem.* You can't sell anything to a prospect who doesn't believe they have a problem.

*Step 2: Quantify the impact of the problem.* The ideal customer's problem is large, complex, and urgent.

*Step 3: Specify the prospect's specific need.* Here you translate the customer's problem into a specific need for your product or services.

*Step 4: Propose your solution.* Your solution must be compelling and easy to understand.

*Step 5: Quantify the benefits you can deliver.* Tailor and dollarize each benefit.

*Step 6: Position your competitive advantage.* Spell out what sets you apart from your competitors.

*Step 7: Substantiate your credentials.* Use testimonials and endorsements to verify your claims.

## The Seven-Step Persuasion Sequence

Weak sales presenters typically miss steps two, five and seven, leaving prospects with concerns and objections. Sellers who miss steps in the persuasion process invariably encounter problems, especially when they are trying to close a big deal.

## STEP 1: IDENTIFY THE PROBLEM

### Finding and Sizing the Problem

> "No pain, no gain; no thorns, no throne; no gall, no glory; no cross, no crown."
>
> —WILLIAM PENN

The first step in a successful presentation is to get agreement on the nature and size of the customer's problem.

Before you start delivering your digital pitch, you should have done your homework and gotten the prospect to share with you what their problems are. Remember, if there is no problem there is no need.

### Visualize the Problem

Use graphics or charts to visualize the prospects problem. You can't solve a problem you can't picture. Keep the graphics simple.

Focus on problems you can solve. Don't develop needs in your presentation for other suppliers to solve. This will simply confuse or distract people.

## Visualizing a Prospect's Problems

In the example below, the presenter is trying to convince the prospect he needs advanced sales training. The problem is highlighted in the prospect's poor skills in four key areas.

The thermometer graph is simple to interpret and persuasive.

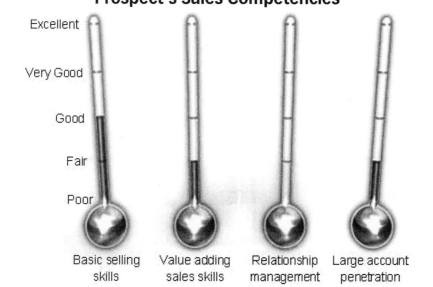

**Prospect's Sales Competencies**

## STEP 2: QUANTIFY THE IMPACT OF THE PROSPECT'S PROBLEM

> "Small problem, small sale;
> Big problem, big sale."
>
> —HARRY MILLS

Prospects won't buy until they fully appreciate the gravity of the problem.

### The Ideal Problem

The ideal problem from a salespersons point of view is:

- **Large:** The bigger the pain, the larger the potential sale.

- **Complex:** Customers pay more to solve complex problems.

- **Urgent:** Prospects who have an urgent problem are less price resistant and have to make a decision quickly.

### Highlight Effects, Consequences, and Impact

Use graphics to highlight the effects, consequences, and financial impact of the problem on your prospect's business.

Involve your audience by asking them what will happen to their business if they don't quickly address the issue you are highlighting.

### Highlight Opportunity Costs

Finally, don't forget to ask what opportunities will be lost if the current business problem remains unaddressed.

## Highlighting the Effect of the Problem

The graphics below clearly show what the implications or consequences are of the poor sales skills highlighted in the previous slide.

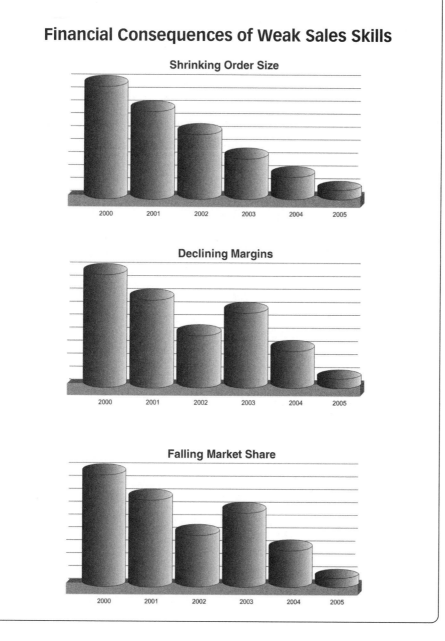

**Financial Consequences of Weak Sales Skills**

## STEP 3: SPECIFY THE PROSPECT'S NEED

### Needs Are Concrete and Specific

"Man is a wanting animal—as soon as one of his needs is satisfied another appears in its place"

—DOUGLAS MCGREGOR

Once you have quantified the impact of the prospect's problem, you are ready to specify what your prospect needs to solve their problem.

The best salespeople incorporate verbatim feedback from their needs analysis into their sales presentations.

In the illustrated example, shown on the opposite page, Jane Asher, the sales director, has declared her problem is that her staff members sell on price. This translates to a *need* to sell value.

CEO Bob Chambers' prime concern is that the competition has better relationships with his clients. This problem translates to the *need* to build complex relationships.

Finally, Marketing Director Peter Climo is concerned about an inability to win big deals. This problem translates to a *need* to win big deals.

PowerPoint allows you to incorporate pictures of your prospects in your slide.

# Linking Problems to Specific Needs

This slide graphically links the various decision makers' actual words with a specific need.

Prospects are invariably impressed when you prove you really have listened to them by taking the effort to quote their actual words. Prospects never argue with their own words.

**Your Needs**

| | Problem | Need |
|---|---|---|
| | "Our people sell on price"<br>**Jane Asher** Sales Director | Sell value |
| | "Our competitors have much better relationships with our clients"<br>**Bob Chambers** CEO | Build complex relationships |
| | "We win very few big deals"<br>**Peter Climo** Marketing Director | Win big deals |

## STEP 4: RECOMMEND YOUR SOLUTION

### Emphasize Practicality

> "There is always an easy solution to every human problem- neat, plausible and wrong."
>
> —H. L. MENCKEN

Customers want practical, credible solutions. So once you have got the prospect to agree to what they need, you are ready to present your solution. The solution is what you are selling.

The solution should emerge as a logical, practical, and credible answer to the problems and needs you have just discussed.

### Make It Brief and Memorable

Keep your approach and recommendations pithy and to the point.

If possible, sequence your recommendations. A three- or four-step solution or approach will help your prospects organize their thinking.

Back up your recommended approach with success stories.

## Presenting Your Recommendations

In the example below, the prospect is being offered a three-step program of sales training. The recommendations follow logically from the previous slides on the prospect's problems and needs.

| Your Needs | Our Recommendations |
|---|---|
| 1. Sell Value | Train all sales staff in advanced customer-driven selling skills program. |
| 2. Build Complex Relationships | Train account managers in strategic account management skills. |
| 3. Win Big Deals | Train key account executives in identifying and winning major sales opportunities. |

# STEP 5: QUANTIFY THE BENEFITS

### Sell the Sizzle

> "There are risks and costs to a program of action. But they are far less than the long-range risks and costs of comfortable inaction."
>
> —JOHN F. KENNEDY

"Sell the sizzle, not the steak." The sizzle is the quantifiable and provable advantage of doing business with you.

Tailor each benefit to your prospect's precise needs. Use the phrase, "you said that" to link the prospect's exact words to your benefits.

### Quantify Each Benefit

Don't exaggerate or oversell. List the key benefits of your recommended solution, and where possible, quantify each benefit. Prospects are looking for quantifiable benefits so make sure you display them.

### Don't Forget the ROI

ROI stands for Return On Investment. Prospects want to see a verifiable return for the money they spend, so wherever possible, quantify:

- The cost reductions you can deliver.

- Likely revenue increases from your solutions.

- Costs the prospect will avoid by adopting your approach.

## Sell the Sizzle

Most prospects like to have their benefits qualified. Qualification of benefit is often an inexact science, so be careful not to exaggerate.

In the case below, the seller uses a survey of 47 clients to justify his figures.

| Likely Benefits from Recommended Training | |
|---|---|
| **Increased Sales** | Average sales for 47 clients increased 8%–28% for 12 months following training. |
| **Higher Margins** | Average sales for sample surveyed increased 12%–32%. |
| **Larger average Size Deals** | Average sized major deals increased 22%–142%. |
| **Reduced Sales Cycle Times** | Clients shortened their sales cycles by 5%–21%. |
| **Short Payback Period** | Average payback period for training: 4.2 months. |

## STEP 6: DIFFERENTIATE YOURSELF

### Don't Ignore Competitors

> "In real estate, its location, location, location.
> In sales, its differentiation, differentiation, differentiation."
>
> —HARRY MILLS

One of the biggest mistakes sales presenters make is to ignore their competitors, to act as though they don't exist.

Don't be afraid to discuss competitors. But always be objective and never exaggerate.

### Highlight Your Strengths

You should never knock your competitors, but you should highlight what makes your solution different and superior.

Spell out what makes your solution different or unique. Position your UVP (Unique Value Proposition).

### Concede Weaknesses

Openly concede areas where your competitors are demonstrably stronger. Open acknowledgment impresses prospects who believe salespeople exaggerate and deceive.

## Differentiating Your Solution

The graphic shown below lists the prospect's decision criteria on the left and rates the Mills Group strengths against their main competitor.

In this example, the Mills Group is clearly weaker than its main competitor in industry expertise. However, the Mills Group is clearly superior in the prospect's top two criteria.

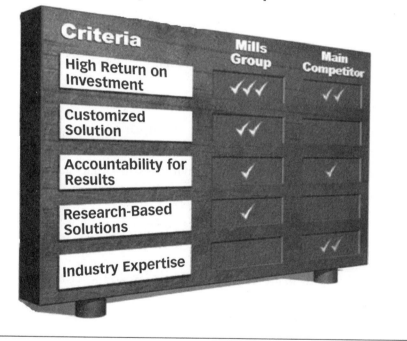

### Why The Mills Group?

| Criteria | Mills Group | Main Competitor |
|---|---|---|
| High Return on Investment | ✓✓✓ | ✓✓ |
| Customized Solution | ✓✓ | |
| Accountability for Results | ✓ | ✓ |
| Research-Based Solutions | ✓ | |
| Industry Expertise | | ✓✓ |

## STEP 7: ESTABLISH YOUR CREDENTIALS

### Verify, Verify, Verify

> "Would you do business with you?"
>
> —LINDA SILVERMAN

President Ronald Reagan, when negotiating with the Russians on nuclear missile deployment, stated "it was never about trust; it was all about verification."

Customers are inherently suspicious about salespeople who exaggerate and misrepresent their services and product.

### Cement the Sale

The purpose of the final step is to cement the sale by providing proof to substantiate all of your claims.

### Use Testimonials and Endorsements

With products such as machinery, its normally easy to verify and test the veracity of your claims. With services, it's much more difficult. This is why you need to provide testimonials and third-party endorsements to demonstrate you have a track record and you can deliver.

### Ask for the Order

Now that you've gone through the seven steps, you are ready to ask for the order.

## Use Third-Party Endorsements

Before you select a third party to endorse your company and deliver a reference, make sure they are someone, or represent an organization, the prospect admires.

In the examples below, the endorsements come from actual clients. The words used are specific and support the seller's claims.

---

## Endorsements

*"Before the Mills Group sales training we closed 1 in 7 proposals. We now win 1 in 3. The deals are bigger and the margins higher."*

Bill Ellison
CEO, Activel International

*"We never appreciated how big a boost to our revenues and margins training could make. In the year following training, revenues increased 28.7% and margins increased 42%."*

Alison Kapel
Sales and Marketing Manager
AMP Technologies

---

# USE A ONE-PAGE VISUAL BRIEF TO CLINCH YOUR SALE

### Create a Visual Executive Summary

Written reports come with their own one- or two-page executive summary, so why shouldn't we also create a visual summary to accompany a major presentation?

To clinch presentations, I like to hand my clients a one-page visual summary of the presentation I've just delivered. An example of a one-page visual brief is shown on the opposite page.

### Laminate Your Visual Sales Brief

Prospects appreciate a one-page visual overview. I also like to laminate my visual brief. The lamination gives prospects the feeling of added value, and decision-makers often toss them into their in-trays when they return to their offices.

The increased win rate that comes from using a visual sales brief more than pays the cost of hiring a graphic artist to design one. At the very least, the use of a visual sales brief also sets you apart from your competitors.

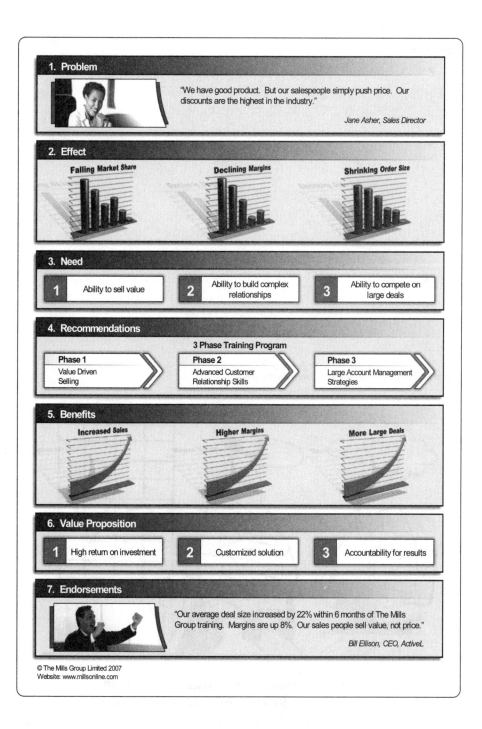

**1. Problem**

"We have good product. But our salespeople simply push price. Our discounts are the highest in the industry."

*Jane Asher, Sales Director*

**2. Effect**

Falling Market Share    Declining Margins    Shrinking Order Size

**3. Need**

1 | Ability to sell value
2 | Ability to build complex relationships
3 | Ability to compete on large deals

**4. Recommendations**

3 Phase Training Program

Phase 1
Value Driven Selling

Phase 2
Advanced Customer Relationship Skills

Phase 3
Large Account Management Strategies

**5. Benefits**

Increased Sales    Higher Margins    More Large Deals

**6. Value Proposition**

1 | High return on investment
2 | Customized solution
3 | Accountability for results

**7. Endorsements**

"Our average deal size increased by 22% within 6 months of The Mills Group training. Margins are up 8%. Our sales people sell value, not price."

*Bill Ellison, CEO, ActiveL*

© The Mills Group Limited 2007
Website: www.millsonline.com

"Fear of public speaking is quite common.
If dressing up as Speaker Man makes you
feel more confident, then so be it."

# APPENDIXES

**Appendix A:** The Mills Persuasive Presentations Formula

**Appendix B:** PowerPoint Presentation Planner Template

**Appendix C:** Blank PowerPoint Presentation Planning Template

**Appendix D:** Organizing Your Presentation

**Appendix E:** Speaker Evaluation Template

**Appendix F:** How PowerPoint 2007 Helps You Create Sensational Presentations

**Appendix G:** Companion CD-ROM

# THE MILLS PRESENTATIONS FORMULA

| The Mills Persuasive Presentations Formula | |
|---|---|
| **PREVIEW** | |
| **1. Hook:**<br>Opening statement to grab attention | _____<br>_____<br>_____<br>_____<br>_____<br>_____<br>_____ |
| **2. Positioning State-ment:**<br>Benefit statement selling advantages of listening | _____<br>_____<br>_____<br>_____<br>_____<br>_____<br>_____ |
| **3. Preface:**<br>Overview of key points | _____<br>_____<br>_____<br>_____<br>_____ |

**VIEW**

**4. Content**

Sell your point of view

Three compelling points
supported by evidence
and illustrations

_____

_____

_____

_____

_____

_____

**REVIEW**

**5. Recap**

Summary of positioning
statement and key points

_____

_____

_____

_____

_____

**6. Conclusion:**

Wrap up story or state-
ment

_____

_____

_____

_____

_____

**7. Call to Action:**

Request for order/com-
mitment

_____

_____

_____

_____

_____

# POWERPOINT PRESENTATION PLANNER TEMPLATE

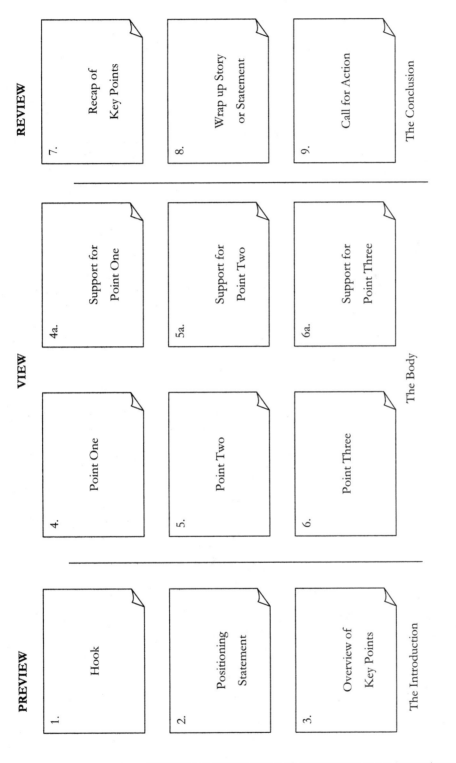

**PREVIEW**

1. Hook

2. Positioning Statement

3. Overview of Key Points

The Introduction

**VIEW**

4. Point One

5. Point Two

6. Point Three

4a. Support for Point One

5a. Support for Point Two

6a. Support for Point Three

The Body

**REVIEW**

7. Recap of Key Points

8. Wrap up Story or Statement

9. Call for Action

The Conclusion

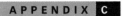

# BLANK POWERPOINT PRESENTATION PLANNING TEMPLATE

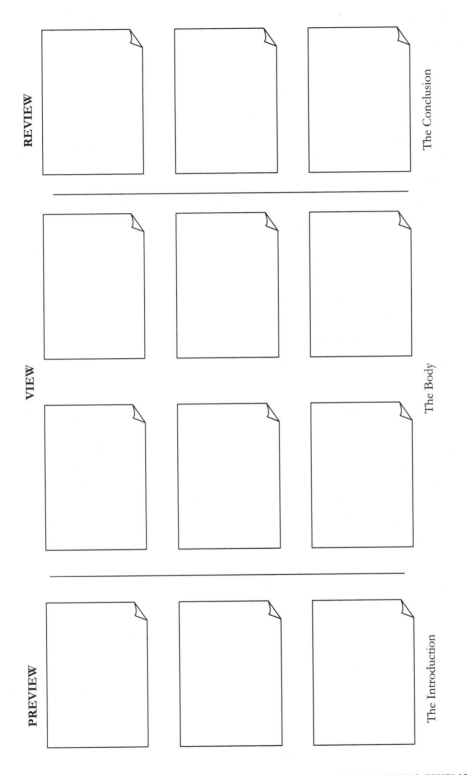

# ORGANIZING YOUR PRESENTATION

Use the presentation organizer below to organize your presentation.

| Presentation Organiser | | |
|---|---|---|
| Topic | Time | |
| Speaker(s) | | |
| Venue | | |
| Address | | |
| Room | | |
| Event Manager | Phone | |
| Room Manager | Phone | |
| Audience Numbers | Room Size | |
| Room/Equipment Checklist | | |
| | ✓✗O | Action |
| Whiteboard | | |
| Flip chart | | |
| Overhead projector | | |
| Markers/tape | | |
| Slide projector | | |
| Film projector | | |
| Videotape player | | |
| Video camera | | |

| | | |
|---|---|---|
| LCD panel | | |
| TV monitor | | |
| Projection screen | | |
| Pointer | | |
| Extension cords | | |
| Electrical outlets | | |
| Extra bulbs | | |
| Lectern | | |
| Microphone | | |
| Chairs | | |
| Tables | | |
| Seating protocol | | |
| Lighting | | |
| Windows | | |
| Acoustics | | |
| Heating/ventilation | | |
| Refreshments | | |
| Phone calls | | |
| Restrooms | | |

✔ = O.K.   ✘ = Needs attention   O = not needed

**Preferred Room Layout (Sketch)**

# SPEAKER EVALUATION TEMPLATE

| Speaker Evaluation | | | |
|---|---|---|---|
| **Speaker:** | | | |
| **Evaluator:** | | | |
| Use the following scale: | | | |
| 1 = Yes    2 = Needs Attention    3 = No | | | |
| **Audience** | | | |
| Tailored to audience | 1 | 2 | 3 |
| Clear purpose | 1 | 2 | 3 |
| Achieved purpose | 1 | 2 | 3 |
| Purpose appropriate for audience | 1 | 2 | 3 |
| **Introduction** | | | |
| Confident speaker | 1 | 2 | 3 |
| Grabbed listener's attention | 1 | 2 | 3 |
| Established need to listen | 1 | 2 | 3 |
| Provided overview | 1 | 2 | 3 |

| **Body** | | | |
|---|---|---|---|
| Easy to follow | 1 | 2 | 3 |
| Clear transitions | 1 | 2 | 3 |
| Compelling evidence | 1 | 2 | 3 |
| Clear memorable points | 1 | 2 | 3 |
| Vivid support (stories, etc.) | 1 | 2 | 3 |
| Persuasive language | 1 | 2 | 3 |
| Established credibility | 1 | 2 | 3 |
| **Conclusion** | | | |
| Summarized key points | 1 | 2 | 3 |
| Memorable conclusion | 1 | 2 | 3 |
| Called for action | 1 | 2 | 3 |
| Handled questions | 1 | 2 | 3 |
| **Visual Aids** | | | |
| Simple view | 1 | 2 | 3 |
| Clear | 1 | 2 | 3 |
| Visible | 1 | 2 | 3 |
| Persuasive | 1 | 2 | 3 |
| Professional look | | | |
| **Body Language** | | | |
| Good eye contact | 1 | 2 | 3 |
| Appropriate gestures | 1 | 2 | 3 |
| Strong confident posture | 1 | 2 | 3 |

| | | | |
|---|---|---|---|
| Professional appearance | 1 | 2 | 3 |
| **Voice** | | | |
| Right pace | 1 | 2 | 3 |
| Clear articulation | 1 | 2 | 3 |
| Correct pronunciation | 1 | 2 | 3 |
| Clearly audible | 1 | 2 | 3 |
| Varied pitch | 1 | 2 | 3 |
| Effective pauses | 1 | 2 | 3 |
| **Suggestions for Improvement** | | | |

_____

_____

_____

_____

_____

# HOW POWERPOINT 2007 HELPS YOU CREATE SENSATIONAL PRESENTATIONS

PowerPoint 2007 allows presenters without any graphics skills training to create high-impact presentations.

## 1. THE REDESIGNED USER INTERFACE MAKES CREATING SENSATIONAL PRESENTATIONS EASIER AND MORE INSTINCTIVE

PowerPoint 2007 has a redesigned user interface with a new look and feel. This makes creating, presenting, and sharing presentations much easier and more instinctive. All the common features you need are a breeze to find and use.

## 2. THE NEW SMARTART FEATURE ALLOWS YOU TO TURN A BULLETED LIST INTO AN IMPRESSIVE 3D SMARTART DIAGRAM

Relationship workflow and hierarchy diagrams have never been easier to create.

## 3. THE POWERPOINT SLIDE LIBRARIES HELP YOU ENSURE THAT YOUR CONTENT REMAINS UP TO DATE

With PowerPoint Slide Libraries, you can easily repurpose slides from existing presentations stored on a site supported by Microsoft

Office SharePoint Server 2007. This slashes the time you spend creating presentations. Slides you insert from the site can be synchronized with the server version so your content is always up to date.

## 4. IN POWERPOINT 2007, YOU CAN DEFINE AND SAVE YOUR OWN CUSTOM SLIDE LAYOUTS

You no longer lose time cutting and pasting your layouts onto new slides or deleting content on a slide with the layout you want. With PowerPoint Slide Libraries, you can share these custom slides with colleagues so that your presentations have a consistent look and feel.

## 5. POWERPOINT 2007 ALLOWS YOU TO CREATE A CONSISTENT LOOK AND FEEL IN ONE CLICK

Changing the theme of your presentation not only changes the background color, but the colors of diagrams, tables, charts, and fonts, and even the style of any bullet points within a presentation.

## 6. YOU CAN EASILY CHANGE SHAPES, TEXT, AND GRAPHICS WITH THE NEW TOOLS TO CREATE DRAMATIC NEW EFFECTS

You'll love the fun and ease you can now have, changing the look and impact of shapes, text, and graphics.

## 7. SPEED UP YOUR PRESENTATION REVIEW PROCESSES USING POWERPOINT 2007 AND OFFICE SHAREPOINT SERVER 2007

It's much quicker with PowerPoint 2007 to accelerate presentation review cycles using the built-in workflow functions in Office SharePoint 2007.

## 8. IMPROVE THE SECURITY OF YOUR POWERPOINT PRESENTATIONS

You can now mark your presentation as final to prevent unwanted changes. Or you can add a digital signature to protect your presentations against unwanted changes. You can even protect and preserve the structure and look of your templates by using content controls.

## 9. REDUCE THE SIZE OF YOUR FILES

The new XML format slashes the size of your files. Smaller file size means you save on storage, and need less bandwidth.

## 10. SHARE FILES WITH USERS ON ANY PLATFORM

You can convert your files to XPS and PDF so you can share them with users on any platform.

# THE COMPANION CD-ROM

Harry Mills with PresentationPro—one of the world's leading PowerPoint design teams—created and designed the model PowerPoint slideshows and templates.

The slideshows provide:

- A series of practical, visual lessons on how to plan, design and deliver persuasive PowerPoints.

- Vivid examples of how spectacular and persuasive PowerPoint can be with the help of imaginative design.

### *Slideshows*

1. **Planning for the Perfect Performance:**
   How to Organize a Persuasive Presentation

2. **Visual Magic:**
   How to Create Stunning Visuals That Sell, Motivate, and Persuade

3. **Wooing with Color:**
   How to Use Color to Enhance, Motivate and Persuade

4. **Deliver with Style:**
   How to Present with Flair and Impact

5. **Stunning Graphics:**
   How to Put the Wow into Pie, Bar and Line Graphs

6. **Dazzling Diagrams:**
How to Inform with Impact

7. **The Ultimate Sales Presentation:**
How to Persuade with Punch, Power and Pizzazz

8. **PresentationPro Templates, Graphics, and Icons:**
Thirty Professional PowerPoint High-Impact Templates
Designed by PresentationPro

# INDEX

decision makers, identifying,
    23
delivery, *see also* body language; voice
    notes used in, 62, 65
    options, 61–63
    rate of, 77–78
    reading a speech, 62–63
    use of pauses, 78
De Man, Paul, 53
diagrams
    adding art to, 145, 146
    marketing strategy, 148
    purpose of, 140
    tips for use of, 140
Disney, Walt, 103
Disraeli, Benjamin, 50, 54
Dwiggins, W. A., 111

echo, 52
Ellison, Bill, 173
Emerson, Ralph Waldo, 121
emotional appeals, 12, 47–48
endorsements, 173
Evans, Harold, 151
executive summary, visual,
    174

fear, as motivator, 13
feedback
    asking friends for, 67

evaluation template, 193
    videotape used for, 67
Fitzgerald, F. Scott, 111
Ford, Henry, 106
Franklin, Benjamin, 53

Gantt charts, 137
Gardner, Herbert, 10
Gettysburg Address, vocal emphasis in, 64
Gibbon, Edward, 157
Glasbergen, Randy, 154
"glittering generalities," 24
goals, realistic, 24–25
Goldwyn, Samuel, 65
Graham, Martha, 72

Halsey, William F. "Bull,"
    147
handouts
    formats for, 65
    speaker notes as, 65
headlines, in PowerPoint presentation, 33–34
Hightower, Cullen, 76
Holmes, Oliver Wendell, Sr.,
    47
humor
    to increase participation,
        155
    myth of, 10
    to persuade, 153
    use of, 11, 39

Image Energy Gauge, 152
information
    need for currency, 38
    relevance of, 43
Instant Calming Sequence
    (ICS), 70, 71


Jackson, Andrew, 91
Johnson, Samuel, 136
Jones, Gerald E., 124, 126,
    132


Kapel, Alison, 173
Kennedy, John F.
    quote by, 168
    rate of delivery, 78
King, Martin Luther
    rate of delivery, 78
    use of alliteration, 52
Kissinger, Henry, 42
Kushner, Malcolm, 153, 155


language
    assertive *vs.* weak words, 76
    persuasive words, 75
    warm *vs.* cold words, 74
Lincoln, Abraham
    Gettysburg Address, 64
    power of three, 56, 57
    stage fright, 69

use of contrast, 52
use of rhyme, 52
Lindberg, Anne Morrow, 117
line charts, 130–131
listening, selling benefits of,
    10
logical appeals, 12, 47–48
Longfellow, Henry Words-
    worth, 39


Macaulay, Thomas Babington,
    44, 47
Mancroft, Lord, 27
Marden, Orison Swett, 66
marketing strategy diagram,
    148
matrix
    purpose, 143
    sample, 144
Mayer, Richard, 92
McGovern, George, 141
McGregor, Douglas, 164
Mehrebian, Albert, 72
Mencken, H. L., 166
metaphors
    defined, 149
    military, 147
    power of, 53–54
    sales funnel, 149–150
    sample, 52
    use of, 20

Mills Presentation Formula,
    181–182
Monroe, Alan, 45
Morrisey, George, 139
motivation
    of audience, 39
    use of fear, 13
Moynihan, Noel, 121
Murray, Patrick, 19
Murrow, Edward R., 12, 69

Naisbitt, John, 128
Nathan, George Jean, 145
Newman, Michael, 59
Nock, A.J., 91
Noonan, Peggy, 51
notes, used in delivery of
    speech, 62

Olivier, Sir Lawrence
    stage fright, 69
    value of practice, 66
opening
    functions of, 36–37
    for PowerPoint presenta-
        tions, 37
    transition to body of presen-
        tation, 41
organizational structure, of
    presentation, 42–43

organization charts
    circular, 142
    purpose of, 141
Orwell, George, 114

Penn, William, 160
perception, speed of, 59
persuasion
    effectiveness of text *vs.* im-
        ages, 118
    motivated sequence, 45
    patterns, 44
    seven-step sequence, 158,
        159
    thoughtful *vs.* mindless,
        118–119
    with visuals, 57–59
    words that sell, 75
Peter, Laurence J., 23
photos
    adding impact with, 151
    using the Image Energy
        Gauge, 152
pie charts, 124–125
Point-Example-Point (PEP)
    formula, 21
power of three, 56–57
PowerPoint 2007, key func-
    tions and benefits,
    197–199

PowerPoint presentation, *see also* presentation
aligned with brain's processing channels, 91–93
avoiding clip art, 98–99
avoiding diagrams, 100
avoiding extraneous information, 98–99
billboard test, 93–94
bullets used in, 114–118
color used in, 108–109
creation of title for, 33
digestible bites used in, 93–94
errors in, 79
graphic organizers used in, 95–96
headlines used in, 33–34
MEGO syndrome, 93
number of slides per, 58, 94
opening for, 37
pace of, 94
planner template, 185, 189
for sequential information, 43
speaker notes for, 65
speaker's position, 78–79
three-act structure, 30–31
tips for, 79, 94
typefaces used in, 111–113
as visual tool, 58, 97
*vs.* speech, 9, 11, 13

practicing
importance of, 66
out loud, 66
for Q&A sessions, 80
presentation, *see also* delivery; PowerPoint presentation; presenting
body of, 38–39
case studies used in, 20, 38
conclusion of, 39–40
delivery options, 61–63
emotion used in, 12
establishing purpose of, 7–9
evaluation form, 84–85
fresh information, 9
highlighting benefits, 13, 36
humor used in, 10–11, 39
internal summaries, 41
logic used in, 12
Mills Presentation Formula, 181–182
opening for, 36–38
organizational structure, 42–43
organizer, 191–192
persuasive, 44–45
quotes used in, 50–51
repetition used in, 10
selling the sizzle, 35
seven steps defined, 5
speech *vs.* PowerPoint, 9, 11, 13

# ABOUT THE AUTHOR

Harry Mills is the chief executive of The Mills Group, an international consulting and training firm. Harry has spent the last 20 years training many of the world's top companies in the art of persuasive presentations.

The Mills Group's corporate clients include IBM, Ericsson, Oracle, BMW, Toyota, Lexus, and Unilever. The Mills Group's professional service clients include the Big Four giants: Pricewaterhouse-Coopers, KPMG, Ernst & Young and Deloitte.

Harry Mills is the best-selling author of twenty five books on persuasion sales and negotiation, including *Artful Persuasion*, *Sales Secrets* and *The Mental Edge*. The American Chamber of Commerce called Harry's book, *Artful Persuasion: How to Command Attention, Change Minds and Influence People,* "one of the best books ever written on persuasion." *CEO Refresher* picked *The Rainmaker's Toolkit* as one of its top business books for 2004.

Harry is also a subject matter expert and mentor for the Harvard Business School Publishing's ManageMentor program on persuasion.

Harry can be reached at harry.mills@millsonline.com.

Further tools, support, and training are available through www.millsonline.com.